MW01488538

1

Home Education for People Who Don't Practice it

A Primer on Home School for Friends, Family, Neighbors, Bosses, and Curious or Opinionated Strangers at the Grocery Store

Lisa Powell

© 2015 Lisa Powell. All rights reserved.

ISBN 978-1-329-32775-7

3

DISCARDED
RAMPART LIBRARY DISTRICT
WOODLAND PARK, CO

Introduction

About five years ago I wrote a booklet called "Type 1 Diabetes for People Who Don't Have It". My young daughter had been diagnosed with Type 1 several years before and I wanted to have something succinct but fairly comprehensive to pass out to folks who were significantly in her life, but not caretakers. The idea was to give folks answers to questions that might be tickling the back of their minds without having every interaction with family and friends wind up being a conversation about diabetes. I self-published in hopes that others might find the booklet helpful, and was gratified to find there were a number of people who seem to have found it of use.

Five years ago my family moved to home schooling our three children. This was not an early decision for us, made with confidence, it was one we inched into after trying many other options. Our oldest had attended four

RANGEVIEW LIBRARY DISTRICT
MAYLAND PARK, CO

different schools – a preschool, a well-rated neighborhood school, a magnet school, a charter school. I myself had taught school before starting a family, and was a substitute teacher afterwards. We were well versed in public school systems but had only outside knowledge of home education.

Like diabetes, the subject of home school can be an awkward one to broach. Outsiders are curious. They have questions they want to ask, but don't know what is appropriate or might be stereotyping. They don't want to offend, and they don't feel they know enough to be sure of avoiding that. They usually have strong preconceptions and no way to evaluate how accurate they are. And they don't want the family to feel like they are only interested in them as some oddity, outliers – defined by their school choice.

Sometimes family or friends can be anxious about the change or the choice. It's unfamiliar territory and they have concerns. Grandparents don't want to interfere, but naturally worry about this new path their grandkids are on. Will the kids be all right? Should I be discouraging this decision or supporting it? Sometimes it's hard for adult children and their parents to discuss the school decision without insecurities getting in the way. I hope this booklet can clear away some of the initial noise so that conversations and observations can become more natural and cooperative.

Other times folks that are on the outskirts of the family life can be curious in more of a friendly, gawking manner. Coaches, employers, coworkers, neighbors – everyone eventually develops an opinion on home education, even if some are tactful enough to keep it to themselves. It can be wearying to find the community passing judgment on your choices, and frustrating when they are doing so with little real information on what those choices look like from the inside. I've often wondered what my neighbors think when they hear my kids out for hours at mid-day jumping on the trampoline – do they figure we never do any academic work? They don't, of course, see us writing and doing math on weekends, late into the evening, even working at night. As home schoolers, one of the perks is that we can enjoy a beautiful day outside because we can adjust our

6

schedule to fit circumstances. But the joy is tinged a little with the worry that we will be misjudged on externals.

This book is written, then, to be a low cost source of basic information on what home education is about and how it works. Hopefully families can use it as part of their toolbox in communicating with their families and communities to make their kids' education plan work. Extended family or friends might themselves find this book and use it to ground themselves in foundation information before starting discussions. In addition, I hope that the smattering of answers here might make it easier for families that are making or considering a transition to home education themselves to discern their paths.

A Note on the Language

To my best knowledge, there is no established politically correct labeling that distinguishes between students whose education is directed immediately by their parents and students whose education is directed through "regular" schooling. In writing this booklet, I've had to accept that any choice of labels will likely get me in trouble with someone. Even the label "home schooled" has its serious problems: first, this kind of education is seldom only conducted in the home; second, the two-word format makes it difficult to use the word in, for example, search engines, but "homeschooled" will always be flagged by your spell check; third, many home schooling parents take grammar very seriously and it will probably make their teeth hurt to see "school" used as a verb.

We have worse problems when we try to figure out what to call folks attending "regular" school. "Regular" seems dismissive and, if you've walked into one of those schools recently, probably fairly inaccurate – same with "normal". "Typical" sounds too clinical, "public" too narrow. I've compromised here by alternating between a word that is probably too flattering and a word that some will find insulting. I talked to a mom once who referred to it as "traditional" schooling. That's hardly accurate, since universal government sponsored education (the bulk of "regular" schooling) is a pretty recent phenomenon. But most modern Americans consider it to be the conservative, traditional approach while home education is the radical or innovating one, so I found it a tame enough term to be used in mixed company when trying not to offend.

"Institutional schooling" is the other term I will use. I am sorry that this term seems pejorative, we tend to think of "institutions" as unhappy places. However, the word is not inherently insulting, and it is a pretty accurate term, as "regular" schooling is that which takes place in institutions rather than in informal or small group environments. Public and private schools are, by definition, institutions. If a reader takes issue with my wording because she doesn't like institutions, I have to suggest that it is the schools, and not my word choice, that she has an issue with.

Using This Booklet

The book is set up with sections addressing the many aspects of home education, and within each section are a number of questions and answers. Feel free to skip about, there is no particular order to the subject listings themselves or to the questions within them. If you are looking for information on a particular subject, the index at the end of the book may help.

Table of Contents

Law

Philosophies

Curricula

Testing and Evaluation

Disabilities and Health

Support Materials

Post-secondary

Socialization

Support Organizations

Why

Perks and Costs

Dad's Point of View

Resource Links

Law

I've put this section right up front, although I find the legal aspects of home education mind-numbingly dull. Feel free to skip it, as I would; but one of the first questions that comes to mind when you hear a family has withdrawn or withheld its kids from public school is, "Is that even legal?"

Legislators face challenges in regulating home education in such a manner that the interests of minors and the public good are protected but the potential of home education isn't arbitrarily limited.

Is home schooling legal in every state?

Yes. Some states are more friendly to home education than others, but all allow it in one form or another.

What kind of variety do you see in the law, state to state?

The Home School Legal Defense Association has a great chart noting the levels of regulation of home education in each state. The Web sites of the various state departments of education usually have information on the law regarding home school.

There is a degree of variation. As an example, Montana law requires parents to notify the county superintendent if their children are educating at home. Students are expected to attend home school a certain number of days each year and cover the basic subjects covered at school, and parents need to keep records on attendance and immunization. But as long as there is no prompt to investigate, the state only interacts with the family at the yearly notification.

Colorado is similar, except that the state requires the notification be sent to a school district – parents can pick their local public or a private or umbrella school to hold their records. Students are also required to take a standardized test or be professionally evaluated every two years so that the state can be sure they are meeting a basic level of education.

Massachusetts, on the other hand, plays out its home school law through a combination of court rulings and local school district policy. Some testing is specifically ruled out of requirement by statute, but other forms of evaluation may be necessary. Parents may need to provide their local school with an explanation of their home school plans.

Then there's Texas. Texas would like you to use books or something like them, really teach your kids and not fake it, and teach them reading, spelling, grammar, math, and citizenship. You're not required to notify or receive approval from any government-run entity.

In all, home school law is an excellent manifestation of the United States' federal system, where the laws of each state reflect the state's traditions, priorities, and character, but where the U.S. Constitution protects the overall right of parents in every state to decide for themselves how their children will be educated.

Who legislates home education, the states or the federal government?

14

State legislatures make laws restricting, regulating, or encouraging home education. The federal government is involved when it becomes necessary to uphold the Constitutional rights of an American citizen – for example, if a state law attempted to abridge a family's right to free exercise of religion through educational choices.

How do nations outside the U.S. handle home schooling? Why is it illegal in some countries?

Home schooling is legal in a large number of nations; again, HSLDA has a comprehensive listing of the legal status of home education in different countries displayed on its Web site. Some nations explicitly allow the practice, others have no compulsory education system so education may be offered but families are not required to use the schools. Some allow it for special situations, or require that all students attend school but don't actively pursue families if they educate at home.

There are some nations that both criminalize home education and actively prosecute those who practice it. Families may be fined, children removed from the home; some families have fled their home countries in order to continue schooling. Germany, for example, claims the state has an interest in keeping its residents and citizens from splintering off into differentiated groups, so they require all children attend German schools. China's public schooling is compulsory, with exceptions made. Sweden is firmly set against home education, and finds it grounds for removing children from the family; Turkish law allows for home schooling parents to be imprisoned.

Why does the law allow home school? Isn't it in the interests of the nation for kids to be educated?

Most folks would agree that all of us benefit from an educated citizenry, but there are many ways to get there. For most of America's history, including the eras when the Declaration of Independence was written and the electric light bulb was invented, compulsory public education was not in force nationally. Through most of history, education was a private matter conducted by families, by hired home educators like governesses, by teachers hired cooperatively by a community (e.g. the one room school house of the prairies), or by religious leaders and schools.

The highly martial Prussian state began educating citizens through government schooling in the 19th century, and the usefulness of a uniform and universal application of education was noted by many who imitated it. Particularly post Industrial Revolution, many saw a consistent education system as important for the development of a strong labor force; others saw the school system as a force for fighting ignorance in a voting citizenry, such ignorance being fatal to a republican form of government.

Today, the wide availability of educational materials and the high education level of many private citizens are often used to make the case that the goals of public schooling may be well or even better served by tailoring and privatizing education programs again. Students schooled privately can access a historically unprecedented depth and breadth of instruction. The best and most widely agreed upon goals of public education – dispelling ignorance, developing skills, passing on cultural knowledge, promoting good citizenship – can certainly now be accomplished through home school. Some goals are less well met. If a public school is meant to also enforce uniformity – in thought, culture, or habit – a home school may not meet this need. Early efforts at compulsory education were in part designed to mitigate the splintering effects of immigration and parochial education. But while home school is not well suited for erasing disparate cultural traditions, it can still be used by parents happy to follow the old "melting pot" ideal, keeping kids informed about their family histories while teaching them to meld in with the American culture in general.

How do truancy laws apply? Who enforces them?

Again, this varies by state. States that require a family notify the state, school, or district when it home schools often require parents to send in their letters of intent before the home school program begins. Once home school begins, if a state requires students school a certain number of hours and/or days the parent must keep track of this time spent. If a family complies with all home school law, though, a student who is not in a classroom is not truant, as she is being fully educated in an alternative, home-based program.

In districts with truancy officers, misunderstandings sometimes lead to interaction between families and the system, which are usually cleared up once the case comes before an authority.

Keep in mind that a child in preschool or early elementary grades may not fall under compulsory education laws at all yet. Some states don't require a child to enter school, for example, until age 7. This means notifications and record keeping for the state do not have to begin until that time. There is also an age beyond which compulsory education is no longer is required, often age 16.

Truancy law is enforced by the local district attorney. Schools can help with tracking and reporting, but school officials have no law enforcement role.

I read in the paper about a case where a child was abused, and the family withdrew the child from the schools in order to hide the abuse. How can the law allow that?

The law does not allow it. These cases are about people committing crimes. They are breaking the law. They break the law when they abuse their child, and they break the law when they try to evade detection.

It is unfortunate that a person might use a facade of home schooling, like she might use a facade of being a good parent or a facade of being a respectable professional, to make it easier for her to commit a criminal act. Before home schooling was widely practiced, abusers might have withdrawn kids from school and moved, or claimed to have moved; falsely claimed to have put kids into private schools; or never enrolled their kids in school in the first place.

We are all obligated to do whatever we can to condemn abuse and forestall it where we can. It's important to remember, however, that these cases are almost never about home school families that abuse. They are about abusers that use home schooling as one of many dodges to avoid detection. When a school, church, or neighbors report suspected abuse, child protection agencies are free to investigate fully even if the parents remove their children from schools at that point. Criminal investigation does not depend on school attendance.

How do I find out what the law is in my state?

The Home School Legal Defense Association has a listing of links for state law, but your state's department of education should be able to refer you to guidelines and even specific state statutes.

What do I do if I think someone is breaking the law?

Where prudent, it is usually a wise policy to ask the family itself if you have questions about the legality of its home school program. Very, very often there is a simple misunderstanding that can be easily corrected. However, if you feel direct contact is ill advised, there are several options.

If you feel there may be some uncertainty, you can contact the department of education, a home school advocacy group, or the school district and ask for clarification of the law before taking action.

If you have reasonable certainty that a law may be being violated, you can contact an administrator in charge of truancy at the local school district, your county's district attorney's office, or the state's office for child protective services if abuse is also suspected. If you are concerned about the safety of the children you should, of course, contact the emergency services of your police department.

Do families have any support if they are falsely accused of breaking the law?

Local home education groups may provide support, and any distance or umbrella programs a family has enrolled in may be able to tangibly support a family by giving evidence of adherence to the law. Other support professionals, like family physicians, may be able to help witness to a family's care, as can neighbors, family, and friends. There are large advocacy groups that will provide legal advice and representation, sometimes without charging a family. However, families always face the possibility of needing to hire legal help to combat a false accusation.

I read of a case where the child protection agency of the state asked to enter a home and investigate the family's school plan, and the family wouldn't let them in. Doesn't that mean they have something to hide? Shouldn't the government be able to enter a home freely, like they can a school?

While home education is a growing movement, it is still one most educators, administrators, and public officials have had little interaction with. Inaccurate preconceptions often spur conflict as more and more families move to an education system still not widely understood by government professionals. When an inquiry or investigation is triggered, it is often wise for a family to slow the process until all parties can move forward in the most productive way.

For example, there could be a case where a school official enters a home and finds no designated place set aside for school, and he then jumps to the conclusion that the family is not educating at all. He may not understand that many families choose to do work in common rooms, or even in outdoor areas or at local cooperative spaces. The entire visit from that point can be unproductive and even adversarial.

If a family is suspected of abuse or crime, law enforcement does have every right to enter and inquire, while respecting all Fourth Amendment rights as in the case of suspected crime in other areas. Warrants, judicial rulings, attorney presence are all part of this process. But an investigation triggered by a reported concern that may or may not have any validity at all does not justify entering a home without permission. Take the example of neighbors feuding over crabgrass or fence lines, with one family escalating the fight by reporting the home schooling family to authorities. If the parents are following all law, educating their children appropriately, and in no way abusing or neglecting their kids, they may well have a conversation with authorities about the situation on their front porch rather than allow a miscreant neighbor to provoke a situation where their children may be frightened and their privacy invaded. Children in public school are not subject to having police or other officials enter their homes and poke through their things where there is no real indication of a crime being committed; home schooled children deserve the same respect.

Have there been any Supreme Court rulings about home education?

The U.S. Supreme Court has never ruled directly on home education as such, but has delivered many rulings that touch on the right of parents to direct their children's education. Most home school law has been played out in lower federal and in state courts.

Is home schooling associated with one political party or the other?

Some folks, particularly in decades past, considered home education a fringe liberal movement, a "hippy" thing. Today many equate home school with conservative Christian families. In both cases, there is usually a good deal of stereotyping and derision involved in the view.

Because of early pioneers that fought for legal protection and laid the groundwork with curriculum choices and formation of support organizations, home education is a very accessible choice today. This means families from all kinds of backgrounds can choose this route if it works for the family. There are no card carrying members of a home schooling party.

Is home education supported by or fought against by public schools and teachers' unions?

There is still often a fairly adversarial relationship between public school institutions and home schooling families. Exiting the system is often viewed as undermining it. In some cases the families that move to home schooling are some of the ones that put the highest priority on education and are willing to devote their time and energy to the endeavor. In a climate where standardized testing determines funding for districts, when students who tend to test well are removed from the district this can create strain. Families sometimes remove to home education after poor experiences with a school, also, so these individual cases can cause friction.

However, many individuals who work in school systems are well aware of the issues the system has, the failings it sometimes displays, and the benefits of individualized education and parent involvement. Good teachers and professionals can often see past the conflicts and give their support to families, or at least to the students themselves. There are also a large number of home schooling families with one parent or another who works or who has worked in public education herself.

Philosophies

One reason families home school is that they find the fairly uniform approach public schools take does not work for one or more of their kids. Maybe the kid does not thrive under the school's philosophies or methods, or maybe the child simply could excel under another umbrella. Parents work hard to find a style and goals that fit the individual child's needs as well as the needs or preferences of the family in general. There are a number of different approaches.

What are learning styles?

There are many different ways in which humans ingest and integrate information, concepts and skills. Each person has strengths and weaknesses in learning. Some kids have a hard time retaining information unless it is written down, others do best with illustrations and diagrams, still others need auditory input – you have to tell them. Some kids are very attracted to tactile input, which may mean they learn best when their senses are engaged, but may also mean they cannot focus well when there are too many sensory stimulants surrounding them.

Kids with attention issues sometimes need to narrow their focus, avoid chemicals and stimulants. Others actually need stimulation to focus – they may use caffeine (not a fabulous choice to have to make, but sometimes a more acceptable stimulant than Ritalin), or they may use adrenaline-inducing frequent deadlines, or work on more than one task at a time. This last tactic seems counter-intuitive; if a student is already unfocused, shouldn't you force him to zoom in on the subject at hand? But kids with attention problems sometimes do much better if you allow them to, for example, listen to a lecture while sketching. Many adults in their work lives intuitively use this tactic, but in a classroom setting this may be too distracting to other students so is often not an option. Kids at home can use this focusing technique if it helps them.

Some students learn best working with other students in small groups; others won't work at all if they are sitting with a friend. Some are right-brain oriented, some left. Some learn best with a structured program with clear expectations and well-defined tasks and goals. Others find such structure stifling and will stall and dodge, only putting full effort into projects they have a hand in choosing and developing.

Parents may choose to play to a kid's strengths and use his learning style for most work, giving him the best shot he can have at learning the material well. Others may decide to challenge a kid to learn using styles he's not already comfortable with.

Traditional school teachers try to individualize programs based on styles, and try to vary the styles they address in the class to give kids with different preferences a "turn". But home education is nicely suited to individualization in a way traditional school simply can't in practicality be.

What are Waldorf and Montessori?

Both are hundred-year-old education models founded largely for the younger crowd but built on philosophies that carry on to later childhood and influence adulthood. They both aim to develop the whole child and both use a great deal of active interaction with a subject – Montessori and Waldorf elementary-aged kids are fairly unlikely to be found at a nailed down desk for predominant chunks of the day.

The Waldorf method focuses on developmental stages and integration. The Montessori method is designed to encourage a child's natural desire to educate, it is a facilitating method of education rather than an overly directing one.

Waldorf teaches educators to be mindful of the beauty of the learning environment; aesthetics are important, as are senses and movement.

Montessori teachers look to open children to their own love of learning. Kids serve themselves and each other at snack time, work in multi-age groups so the youngers can learn from the olders, have choices in activities and develop preferences and self-direction in learning.

These methods have been extensively developed and there is a huge degree of support and loads of resources for parents trying to move down either path. In many ways, these sorts of philosophies were the precursors for much of modern home education because although classroom teachers worked the programs, the approach varied substantially from the common classroom experience.

What is STEM?

STEM is an umbrella term referring to a clump of related subjects – science, technology, engineering, and mathematics. Recent concerns about employment and global competition have encouraged institutional school planners to look again at how to nail down competency and encourage excellence in these areas.

The drive is similar to the one that addressed the problem of functional illiteracy in this country some decades ago.

Home school families are also sometimes intensely interested in supporting STEM education for their kids, and may home educate specifically in order to focus on those areas.

What is living history or living books?

A living text approach uses "real" books in instruction, rather than textbooks and readers. The idea is that people naturally learn best by reading a volume written by a person with specialized independent interest on a topic, not by reading books from textbook publishers written specifically as summaries for a classroom.

"Living books" is one important component of Charlotte Mason education.

Historical fiction, fictionalized biography, or narrative geography are sometimes used in a living history program. Students may be given a backbone of history of an era or geographic area through lecture, timeline, or written summary and then read a large number of story-based books that flesh out the time and place.

Elementary students studying ancient history and biology might use biographies and story books on Romulus and Remus and the emperors, and a quality kids' account of the ancient mythologies, rather than a history text about ancient cultures. They might read story books about biology, such as the Magic School Bus series, or books on the planets by Seymour Simon, rather than have a general science book with a multi-subject format and a grade level designation. They will read Milne's Pooh books or Beatrix Potter's rabbit stories instead of selections written specifically for a reader.

Older students studying the same subjects might read speculative fiction about ancient Rome, Greece, Sumaria, Egypt, Persia, and Judea. Biology might be studied reading narratives about Jane Goodall's work or the life of Henrietta Lacks or Clara Barton. Literature would include short stories, essays, poetry and novels, as well as nonfiction works like travelogues or political or social commentary. Again, the standard unwieldy textbooks would not be the primary method of gathering information, although they can be used as a reference or a primer to build a living books curriculum upon.

What is a great books program?

The 1920s saw a movement that included public intellectuals such as Mortimer Adler and John Erskine that promoted the reading of great Western classics as a comprehensive approach to education. This was in contrast with much of the professionalized education approach advanced by public education founding fathers like John Dewey.

An example of a great books program is that of St. John's College, where students study work by Homer, Locke, Socrates, Plutarch, Marx, Lincoln, and others. Many great books schools provide book lists on their Web sites that home school families can plunder for suggestions.

Many home educators use a variation on great books studies. One advantage is that materials are often in the public domain or can be borrowed from the public library or purchased used.

The great books approach is not limited to the liberal arts, math and science are also taught using original sources such as Euclid and Darwin.

What is the difference between a "great book" and a "living text"?

There isn't always a difference, there can be crossover between the two areas.

In general, though, the great books are considered founding classics in the fields they enlighten. A "great book" in mathematics might be Euclid's *Geometry*. A closer fit for a living text might be something like the *Murderous Maths* series, the *Life of Fred* series, or Terry Jones's video series on the history of numbers. A book like *Flatland* would be in a fairly grey area – it is certainly a living text, but by our time it could also be considered a classic and nearly a great book.

Both approaches take the point of view that kids should read books written for the world, not solely for a classroom.

Who was Charlotte Mason, and what does she encourage?

Mason was an educator who wrote books discussing her understanding of education at the turn of the 19th century. Her ideas have bled into a lot of different home school approaches – it would be difficult to find one that didn't share some of the ideas she developed. There is quite a bit to learn from her, and many families are Charlotte Mason all the way – but others incorporate part of her philosophy into their program.

Her ideas include interaction with and writing about nature; a disciplined approach to schooling; a belief in the inherent educability of all children; segmented learning units of limited length; the use of living books and narration; and the provision of a "generous" curriculum for children to indulge in.

What is unschooling?

Unschooling is one of those terms whose definition varies by user. The essence of unschooling is the attempt to shake learners and teachers out of the assumptions and habits they unself-consciously have adopted and persisted in. Practices are all laid out and reconsidered fresh before they are either continued, modified, or trashed and replaced.

An almost universal belief of unschoolers is that learning is part of human nature and that adults who want young people to learn largely simply need to get out of the way. "Schooling" can actually kill or corrupt the instinctive, healthy desire to accumulate knowledge and understanding – we've all seen examples in kids who love a subject until they enter a classroom where they are told they have to study the subject in a way the teacher randomly prefers.

Most unschooling families believe in a degree of student-led learning. Options are presented and students will choose from them, often reaching competency levels they would not have achieved if they'd been compelled to follow a path chosen by someone else. Parents and other mentors act as facilitators and resources, not normally directly as teachers.

Often other aspects are nontraditional, also – for example, students may learn outdoors rather than in a classroom, at night instead of during a standard school day, or through apprenticeships instead of textbooks.

Self-described unschooling families are wildly different from each other. Some are very determined about their choice, others fell into the practice simply by their nature. Some are very interactive and others have each child working independently much of the time. Some devote huge amounts of time to traditional subjects but vary the way those subjects are learned; for others, subject matter is negotiable also. If you find a student who does little that is recognizable as schooling except reading library materials he has chosen himself and who spends much of the day socializing in different venues, you may be seeing an unschooler. If you find a student who has decided he will work on nothing but math, moving from pre-algebra to calculus in six months, you may also be visiting with an unschooler.

What is the Trivium and a classical education model?

The classical model is a traditional approach that uses much of the pedagogy of schools before the 1950s, when primary and secondary education followed a different and in some ways more rigorous pattern. In contrast with modern teaching approaches, which often race into the higher levels of the education pyramid (the pyramid is often drawn as moving, from bottom to top, from knowledge to comprehension,

39

application, analysis, synthesis, and evaluation), classical education works to build a solid base, thoroughly inform students, and solidify an ability to think before moving on to higher forms of learning.

Classical education is more likely to incorporate scholarly languages (such as Latin, Greek, or Hebrew) and often includes music instruction. Students who use these subjects to learn how to learn then have the skills to tackle other subjects thoroughly in future.

Trivium programs work from the understanding that children grow in and out of developmental stages over the years. Children and young people at different stages are inclined to learn in different ways, and a good program tailors the instruction to fit these stages. Home Trivium programs lead children through the grammar stage in elementary years, the dialectic stage in adolescence, and the rhetoric stage as teens and young adults. Each student, of course, will move out of one stage and into the next at different ages, but general guidelines are given.

Families who use these models often use a great deal of support material and associate in classical communities, it is a rigorous approach that takes a good deal of planning and time but can yield spectacular results. Students led through these programs are often very well equipped for future study.

What is the Robinson curriculum? A Thomas Jefferson Education? Easy Peasy?

There are dozens, if not hundreds, of smaller home education models searching families can find. Modern home education now has over 40 solid years under its belt and in that time many groups and families have innovated directions and resources and made them available – sometimes commercially, sometimes voluntarily – to families that follow.

Thomas Jefferson Education (TJE), for example, is a mentor-based approach that attempts to simulate the kind of education the early American educated class received – independent study under the guidance of specialists in their areas of study.

The Robinson curriculum is based on the collection of Dr. Art Robinson, a widower who improvised a way to continue his work while home schooling his six children. The curriculum is based on "self-teaching" with heavy desk work, and is suited to math and hard science instruction.

The Easy Peasy Web site is one family's home instruction program posted for the use of others. It has a Christian foundation and makes good use of internet resources.

None of these approaches is a universal fit, one of the strengths of home education is that a family can pick one or more approaches that are good for it rather than try to adapt to one nationwide model.

Why do some families incorporate the courtship model in their schooling?

The older school years are often years where relationships have potential to develop, both friendships and the beginning of interest in romantic relationships. Generally, cultural cues are the guide for young people in this area but some families feel the white noise of our current culture makes it difficult for some to hear healthy cues clearly. Many programs have been written to help teens navigate relational waters, and some promote a "courtship model" (a holistic and purposed approach to relationship building) rather than a dating model.

"Teaching" a courtship model is not really that different from mom and dad giving dating advice under other circumstances – parents talk to their children, pass on their views and advice, sometimes have them read material on the subject or listen to or read anecdotes about courting. Families may arrange meals, dances, or other social events within the home school community or within a church or neighborhood community in order to make this transition to adult peer relationships smoother.

How about homes that stress art, outdoor activities, music, languages, or vocational studies?

One of the greatest perks of home education is the potential for individualization; another is efficiency. When you put these together, what some families find is that they can fit seven hours of traditional academics into four or fewer hours and then use the extra hours in the day to concentrate on a specialized field of study. After covering the "basics" a student may have time to write a novel, repair a car, create a documentary or a number of paintings for a local art display. Students in traditional education also specialize, of course, but home education can make it easier.

It can sometimes create concern when a student is very intensely working on a side vocation; a teen who spends five hours a day on gym practice might trigger worry that she's not "doing any school". Remember that writing, reading, math, history, science may all be finished for the day before gym even starts – or the student might work evenings, weekends, or nights on her standard schoolwork. Some alter the typical vacation schedule, schooling during others' spring, winter, and summer breaks and taking their time off during competitions, performances, or workshops.

Curricula

Like geese honking into a din as they crowd about by a lake, when home school moms get together the call of "So, what curriculum do you use?" fills the air. Exploring curriculum options is one of the fun parts of home school, although it can also be one of the expensive parts. Some families purchase a boxed curriculum and follow it in each grade, for all subjects, to the letter. Others pick and choose from different programs to develop their own plan for each kid.

What is a boxed curriculum?

Boxed curricula can be a good choice for parents who'd rather not reinvent the wheel. A mom who has supportive financial resources but little time (or natural inclination) for planning and for collecting materials may want to search the boxed options to see what pre-packaged program best fits her needs. These programs usually cover every subject area over a set of school years. Some provide all materials in a consistent format – their own texts, workbooks, testing materials, answer booklets, and sometime audio or video supplements. Others provide a framework and a suggested list for texts – for example, many will suggest using a pre-existing program for math.

Some families find structure, discipline, and consistency by using these sets to the letter with each home schooled child; others use the boxed set as a foundation and tack on other programs or skip the parts of the set that don't fit the year.

I keep hearing about Sonlight, how does it work?

Sonlight is a company that packages Christian education programs for each grade level. It's a lightly great books program that gives step by step instruction on how to teach all regular subjects and recommends books for use; you can buy the books as part of the package. Sonlight is good for folks who like organization and consistency, particularly from year to year. Families with more than one student can use much of the purchased material for several children over the years.

What does Apologia offer?

Apologia is a science curriculum created by Jay L. Wile. The extensive set of textbooks, workbooks, lab workbooks, lab kits, and testing materials is designed to be used from elementary grades through high school and to give students a rigorous science education in a way that does not discount or disrespect faith. The books teach from a creation science foundation and that perspective is consistent throughout; however, much time is also spent teaching competing theories so students are fully informed about current thinking from all directions.

Christians whose theology calls for a literal Bible interpretation often find conflict in secular texts and testing because the material seems to them to promote a world view rather than simply teach scientific theory. Many text sets require, to one degree or another, that testing students not just understand the material but affirm a belief system. This can be a source of constant and distracting tension, so the Apologia program can allow these families to deeply explore biology, zoology, botany, physics, and chemistry without being constantly abraded.

Folks without this theological view often also use Apologia products because they are known to be very strongly academic and highly structured. The chemistry program for high school, for example, is extremely math centered. The textbooks for general science and above include instructions for labs.

What is in Ellen McHenry's basement?

You may already be familiar with McHenry's work from her illustrations for Dover books, including activity books for children. She has independently developed several different subject packets for science and geography. Her *Mapping the World with Art* program takes students step by step through freehand drawing of the world, and includes a geography textbook with optional activities.

McHenry has thin texts for botany, cells, and the brain. She has descriptive chapters, varied activities, and links to internet resources for each of these. She's also collaborated on texts for other subjects. Buyers can download extensive samples for most of her works.

My local public school offers Lincoln Interactive. What's that?

Lincoln is one of several full programs public school systems use with folks who want to school through a district but outside the classroom. Students might use home computers, lab computers, or use a book system at home. Often the district will provide support staff that families can contact for help reaching the goals of the program. Generally, folks using these programs use them like boxed curricula, using Lincoln for every subject area. There may be a requirement that a certain portion of activities and work must be completed by the end of the school year.

What math programs are out there, and which is best?

Some of the main math programs are Math U See, Singapore Math, Saxon Math, Math Mammoth, Teaching Textbooks, and VideoText.

Saxon is probably the one most widely used program for home schoolers; inclusive programs often tack Saxon on as their math. Saxon has a solid history in and out of schools, and it has a line of products specifically designed for home education. Advanced levels can include video instruction. All levels have student texts, workbooks, testing materials, and answer keys. Early grades have flash cards and other simple hands-on materials. Saxon Math is based on a spiral approach. Each lesson teaches one discreet task, and is followed by a set of problems implementing that lesson. There is then a second set of problems that provides practice for that task and for tasks from previous lessons. Very frequent testing also reinforces previous lessons. Saxon is practice intensive and walks students through a lesson step by step; there is a lot of repetition and it can feel very stilted. It is also fairly heavily language-oriented, with instruction being descriptive as much as demonstrative.

Math U See is more focused on manipulatives and hands-on learning, with computer applications supplementing. Singapore associates itself with the math teaching methods used in Singapore and other East Asian countries that have a solid track record on mathematics testing. Teaching Textbooks is an internet interactive program with instruction, practice, testing, and feedback; later versions' automatic grading and explanation for problems worked in error can take the pressure off parents to address math difficulties. VideoTexts is an older, tested program with video lessons followed by worksheets and quizzes, all in small bites.

The Math Mammoth program is a full math instruction course developed by Maria Miller. Miller has several videos on YouTube explaining parts of her instruction, and you can access samples and information on her books and supplements at her Web site. Math Mammoth allows you to purchase books as downloads or on CDs, printing copies at home for different children as they get older. This can be a real money saver. She also allows you to follow the math program grade by grade or topic by topic. Math Mammoth is colorful and largely self-teaching for good readers, threading instruction into the packet of problems. It does have a large number of problems to work each day.

The major home school boxed programs, like A Beka, have their own math programs you can use. Rod and Staff publishes a math program that is practically oriented, delivering solid math instruction ending in math for business or life rather than higher maths for those who intend to seek a bachelors in science in college.

There is no one "best" math program, many excellent results have been seen with each of the above and others. Families generally select a math program after some trial and error to see what best fits the students' learning style, the parents' teaching preferences, and the rest of the home program and schedule.

What is A Beka?

A Beka is a Christian textbook company that provides colorful texts in many subject areas, including mathematics and phonics, for home educating families. It is relatively easy to use and has a solid history in teaching the basics.

What is My Father's World?

My Father's World is a program based on developmental levels. It's a Christian curriculum particularly designed to be used by families simultaneously teaching a number of students with moderate to small age gaps. Students can all use the same resources while investigating the subjects at greater or lesser depth, depending on age and ability level. This is handy for parents, who can complete much of the school day communally and then break off for individual work, rather than try to have whole separate programs for the five year old, the seven year old, the nine year old, and the eleven year old.

Who is Susan Wise Bauer, and what does Peace Hill Publishing offer?

Bauer is the writer of *The Well Trained Mind* and one of the early resuscitators of a classical, trivium-based model. After developing methods of teaching her own children she created a line of products that can be strapped together (with some extras, like a math curriculum, added in) to develop a full home program. Her book explains how to assemble your own plan, but her other resources can help shortcut the process.

Peace Hill Press offers a grammar program with a scripted method that walks you through parts of speech, diagramming, etc. Her method puts a great deal of emphasis in early years on memorization, narration, and dictation. Kids learn to recite great works of poetry as well as to comprehensively read and retell samples.

One of Peace Hill's most widely used products is her four part book series, *The Story of the World*. Bauer's curriculum recommendations are based on a four year cycle. Students in science, for example, will study chemistry, physics, biology, and geology and astronomy in four separate years, and then repeat the cycle at a greater depth again and again. In history, she breaks the program into the ancient, medieval, early modern, and modern worlds, and then suggests repeating that cycle twice with greater depth. The SOTW history series can be used as a backbone for this method; it delivers a broad, general world history with a Western emphasis but a global reach. The series is available in abridged form in audio – downloads or CDs. Families can read the accessible books out loud, have students read themselves, or have students listen individually or during "car schooling" – while traveling or driving to activities.

Is Rosetta Stone the only language program out there?

Rosetta Stone is a tested and well-loved program with many languages to choose from. It is designed to bring students to a level of competency few other autopilot programs can reach, but it still takes commitment and it can be pricey. Some libraries offer access to Rosetta or other language programs through language or computer labs or home school resource rooms. Alpha Omega also has several computer programs to teach the more common foreign languages.

Students who are just looking to begin study or to get a general familiarity with a language can use more commercial programs like the Talk Now! Series, the Muzzy series, or old standards like Berlitz.

Classical languages and Hebrew often have intensive learning programs of their own. Latin, for example, can be taught well using the

Cambridge series. Home schooling families can also simply buy textbooks and packages from textbook publishers if the parents already speak the foreign language themselves, or if they can find a mentor who does.

What is a CLEP?

Parents of college-bound kids, or potentially college-bound, may use CLEP preparation books and programs as their kids move into high school. Others can use CLEP prep as a simple way to build a transcript.

The College Level Examination Program is administered by the same folks who run the Advanced Placement (AP) system. High school students or graduates can study independently subjects from literature to biology to algebra and then take a test through CLEP. The test evaluates whether the student has learned enough to pass a general education college class in that subject area. Not all colleges and universities accept CLEP results, but some will allow a CLEP test to substitute for a class requirement. CLEPing is one way to reduce college costs, as students can sometimes complete a year of courses through testing at a substantially lower cost. Other students may use the CLEP results as a transcript boost on college or job applications.

Are those the only options?

There are dozens, if not hundreds, of curriculum aids on the market. It's a wide open field being entered by more and more fun and interesting entrepreneurs every day.

Does care need to be taken in selecting a curriculum?

Most families find selecting material to be a fun part of home school planning – it's the Christmas part, where you go to the mailbox and collect a package with a bright, shiny set of new books. But it can become daunting, trying to find the "perfect" set of materials for each schooling child. It's good to remember not to make the perfect the enemy of the good; that you are likely to find you have to discard one or more hopeful directions before finding the right one; that even when you find the "right" curriculum you may eventually have to move on to another; and that a solid education can usually be had from most of the standard programs out there, particularly if you supplement the curriculum with activities, classes, trips, groups, and reading material and games.

New families should be aware that the home school market has become a hot one, and there are folks out there not well versed in the needs of home education who want to throw out products and programs quickly to capture dollars. Parents should beware programs advertising automatic miracle results. If family and friends hear of promising programs and materials they should feel free to mention them to home schooling parents, but don't be disappointed if they don't adopt them, choosing materials is a complicated and individual process.

Can you just use standard textbooks like schools use?

Yes. The major textbook companies have Web sites that will give you information on what their current lines are and how they fit grade levels. Be aware that a home schooled student may not fit perfectly into a school grade level, so parents may need to purchase texts from lower or higher grades than the age of their student would suggest. Also available are teacher editions of the textbooks, which can walk a parent through the text and give him confidence he is teaching accurately.

This direction can be very pricey, as individual purchases won't have a group discount.

Parents who choose the school text option should consider used books stores and outlets such as Abebooks. Buying an edition from a year earlier can be cost saving. It's also sometimes useful to use, maybe as a supplement to another program, old textbooks from past decades. Mathematics teaching, for example, is very subject to trends and some students may learn better using the math teaching from the '80s, or even the '50s. Be sure students who use these texts know how to complete today's standardized math tests correctly, though – some may grade based on method used as well as on the accuracy of answers.

Do you have to use a curriculum?

Absolutely not. Many, even the majority, of families do not use one complete package program for their schooling. Often a family will use a combination, eclectically picking and choosing for each child. For example, a student might use *First Language Lessons* from Susan Wise Bauer for grammar, an Abeka book for math, Our Father's World for history, Apologia for science, and a variety of library-borrowed living books for literature.

How do folks afford all that?

A family can certainly break the bank on materials. There are ways to economize.

Trying out the programs before buying is important. Parents can talk to other families to get personal accounts of the usefulness of materials, or join forums like the Well Trained Mind forum and ask questions. Many programs will send samples, or feature downloadable previews, and those should be taken advantage of. Used book stores and libraries may have pieces of curricula, sometimes outdated or marked, but still useful for evaluation.

Once a family is ready to purchase, finding a home school group and joining in on a curriculum buy/ swap can save money. Families with older students often can sell or give away their old books and disks, which tend to accumulate and take up a lot of household space. Public libraries sometimes have a home school section where material can be checked out for six months at a time. If a family is in crisis or has experienced a financial hardship, like a job loss, some companies have programs that discount materials; the scholarship-like programs may not be advertised but can be available to those who ask and qualify.

Above all, parents need to never fall into the trap of believing only one solution is available for education materials. Often the trade is money against time and effort – most subjects can be taught with little purchased material if a parent rolls up her sleeves and digs into free resources from the Internet, from libraries, and from life. The more expensive materials are designed to make home education easier, and are priced accordingly, but they aren't required to make it possible.

Testing and Evaluation

Home schooled students normally need to pass tests and have their work evaluated, but the systems for doing so are not as set in stones as those in public school. Parents are not as restricted by testing requirements, but also have to work a bit harder to get proper evaluation completed because they are outside the system. Extended family is often interested in test results and other forms of evaluating progress – aunts and grandparents want to make sure their nieces and grandsons aren't falling behind.

How do home school students do, as a population, on standardized national tests?

This can be a hard question to answer for several reasons. First, there are different kinds of standardized tests with different goals. Tests such as the California Achievement Test, the Iowa Test of Basic Skills, and the now-developing Common Core-based tests are not designed to evaluate the performance of individual students, but of a population of students within an institution. They are tests of the quality of the schools and their staffs, not of the achievements of students. These tests are used to reward achieving schools, teachers, and administrators and to identify problem schools, teachers, and administrators.

Other nationally administered tests, like the SAT and ACT, GRE and GED, are designed to evaluate individual students' abilities. These tests are used to determine placement and grant and scholarship eligibility.

So the question is twofold, really. Do home school students as a population generally test in a way that identifies their "schools" (their home educators) as competent? And additionally, do home school students as often as institutionally schooled students individually test well enough to place well and receive grants and scholarships?

For populations, the answer is certainly yes to both questions. The average SAT score for home schooled students who take the test is higher than the general average. Scores on standardized tests such as the CAT normally show a higher average for home education than for institutional schooling. The Home School Legal Defense Fund site has statistical information on testing that confirms that testing shows home education to be on average not just of equal quality to institutional academics, but often of higher quality.

Of course, statistics are never the end of the story. Some states don't collect information on home schooled students' tests, and some home students (just like some traditional students) do not take optional tests such as the SAT. Public school advocates often argue a selection bias in the home school population, they contend that the families that home educate tend to be the ones with the resources and will to devote to the endeavor, so that the very poor or those families who do not highly value education tend to be disproportionately over-represented in public schools. How that affects the stats, though, is difficult to assess – the argument is essentially that home students test better because they have more incentive and support for learning, which doesn't really negate the fact that they do, in fact, test better.

It's hard to say with certainty that the statistics are highly useful here, but it can be a comfort for families and friends to know that the best information we have shows that home schooling delivers an equal or higher level of academic product than traditional schooling.

Are there special challenges with testing and home school?

There are.

Schools are highly motivated to score high on standardized tests, as those tests are evaluating the schools and money is often tied to success and improvement. Schools then are tempted to "teach to the test" – devote much time during the school year to teaching specifically those subjects and skills the teachers and administrators know will be tested for. Other areas may be neglected, leaving students with a poorer education but better test scores. Home school families wish to evaluate well on these tests, but there is no money attached to high scores and low scores normally punish only by forcing the parent to re-enroll her children in school. That is a strong motivating factor in itself, but usually only kicks in if a child scores very low on a test – essentially, if he is failing badly. Most parents do not need to "teach to the test" to avoid that, they simply teach a regular school year.

Home students sometimes, but not always, also test less often overall than institutionally schooled students. In a classroom setting, teachers rely on regular quizzes and testing to be sure students are on track; but one on one learning means this kind of evaluation feedback at home is immediate and ongoing. A parent doesn't need to test as often, because she can see as the subject is being learned where the holes and misses are and address them in real time. This doesn't mean home schooling skips testing – particularly in subjects such as math, testing can lend an objectivity and is very useful. But it usually doesn't happen as often. Home students, then, are often not as adept at actual test taking skills – they may need instruction on filling in the little circles properly, or on how to eliminate options on a multiple choice quiz, or on whether a specific test is the kind that you should include "best guesses" for or leave a question unanswered if you aren't certain.

Parents also face challenges with standardized testing. Home educators may be required to test or may test voluntarily to inform themselves about how their program is proceeding, but they have to seek out methods of testing by themselves. Teachers and schools have the package automatically fitted for them, but a home educator needs to find one of several companies that provide testing material or find a center (in a school district or with a private home school association or co-op) that will administer tests. Schools generally test at a set time each year, nationally uniform (this is one reason why public schools recently had a rash of ending the year later and later; as schools were compared with their peers across the country they changed their schedule in order to get in the maximum number of instructional hours before the set testing dates). Home educators often feel the need to test in the same window (or actually are required to by circumstance), so, like the schools, they may feel the need to adjust their school year around testing. This is a particular problem, though, for folks who home school because they need an altered schedule (e.g. athletes, traveling families, families that school best by working fewer hours each day but working year-round, etc.). Those families may decide to take the hit on test scores rather than make schedule changes, testing for the year before they actually finish the year.

None of this constitutes any kind of undue burden, it's just the vagaries of life. But it might be taken into account when discussing any one student's testing record.

What kind of evaluations don't use formal testing?

Some states allow a qualified person to evaluate a student's performance in lieu of testing. There are normally regulations regarding this process, which some families find gives them more specific information than standardized testing does.

How do you know the parents aren't cheating when they test their kids?

Because parents often administer standardized tests themselves, or select their own evaluating parties, it's fair to question whether the results of those tests aren't often altered. Do the parents coach the kids? Do they follow the instructions for administration to the letter? In short, can they cheat?

Worries can generally be set aside for home schooled students as a population. America has had several generations of home education now. These students have moved on to attend college at many levels, attend vocational school, enter professions and take jobs. If students were wholesale falsely testing as competent, the problem would have been detected by now. Overall it seems likely that parents test their kids honestly.

But for any one student, care must be taken. A parent administrating the test has to be careful to scrupulously follow instructions. The tests, even if given at home, are always graded by an outside agency. Parents must be diligent about test marking and the accompanying paperwork. Many home school parents want the best possible information from standardized tests, because the tests can help them identify weak spots in their program that they can then address. They want accurate testing as much as the state does. Often they will use an outside testing center – like a public school or cooperative that offers testing. This provides complete objectivity, an unimpeachable test result, and gives students practice in institutional testing situations.

Is it possible, though, for parents to rig a test and turn in false results? It sometimes is possible. It's important to keep in mind that standardized tests are not really about evaluating the student's performance. That's the job of exams, quizzes, and tests given in the classroom based on the school year and texts. Standardized testing in schools and at home are designed to evaluate the quality of the teaching. If a whole family fails to reach the designated score on these tests, the family may be required to return its kids to public school.

However, the same "incentive to cheat" works on the public school teacher and the school administration. Federal funding is often tied to improved school performance on these tests. Teacher salaries often are linked to test scores of the kids in their classrooms. Parents may be tempted to cheat in order to keep home schooling, but school staff may be

71

similarly tempted to cheat to receive more money. Teachers and administrators indicted in the Atlanta testing scandal in 2015 demonstrated that school staff are capable of cheating on standardized testing.

Standardized testing is an imperfect tool, subject to corruption, but that's not a home school thing.

How do you keep yourself honest and objective in evaluating your child's progress, strengths, and weaknesses?

Each family has to tackle this one in its own way. Parents are aware that while one on one instruction means immediate and detailed feedback, being "too close" can cloud vision, also. Testing and extracurricular activities are useful for checking assumptions. For example, a student who seems to struggle in geography but wins his local home school geography fair prize might be re-assessed by a parent as being anxious from perfectionism rather than confusion.

My friend teaches her kids at home, they never seem to take tests. Is that normal?

It can be pretty normal.

Remember, a teacher with twenty to thirty kids in a classroom must find a way to make sure those kids are on the same page before she moves on. She simply doesn't have the time to work with each kid, ask him to do problems or read selections and answer questions verbally, every time a new section is tackled. Evaluating a class of 25 kids this way, assigning ten minutes for each mini-conference, would take five or six full school days. Tests and quizzes are essential, all students evaluate concurrently and the tests can be graded outside the school day.

But at home, the educator works with the student on each subject and gets immediate input on whether the subject is mastered or not. In those areas where the student works independently, an evaluation can be informal and verbal – "Tell me how to calculate a mole of sodium".

Paper testing has its place, and some families use it regularly, particularly in subjects such as math. But it's bound to be used less at home than in an institutional school.

Recall also that you, as an outsider, probably never see either home students or public schooled students testing, you are probably simply remembering that you took frequent tests in school yourself.

Do home schooled kids have to take the national standardized tests like everyone else?

This depends on state law, but many do, or need some other form of evaluation, at least in rotating years.

Students who wish to apply to programs or to college need to take the same tests (such as the SAT) that all others in that situation take.

How do home educators acquire standardized testing materials?

There are several companies (Christian Liberty Press and Seton Testing are two) that sell testing services. You can access those services online. The companies will guide you through selecting the best tests, mail you packages with instructions for administration and the student booklets and answer sheets. Students complete the test and the entire package is mailed back to the company, which then grades the sheets and sends the results.

These tests are often old editions of regular standardized tests used in public schools. The current editions cannot be use for the sake of security, but older editions can be. The California Achievement Test, the Iowa Test of Basic Skills, Stanford tests and others are available. Generally, the older tests my be more difficult than the newer versions, so there is generally not a concern about using the alternative versions.

Parents also can inquire with local public schools or public charter schools to see if their kids can sit in on the testing the school must do each year. Some enrichment programs also offer testing days.

Disabilities and Health

Schools are usually characterized as academic or even social environments, but in recent decades they've been more and more tasked with evaluating and promoting physical health in students. Many feel home school needs to match that aspect of schooling as well, and are concerned about how health, nutrition, and activity needs can be met outside a school setting.

How do kids get evaluated for disabilities if they are at home and don't have contact with early intervention specialists?

Most states require that public school specialists be available to home school families for evaluations. This makes immediate sense; if the state system is charged with educating all the state's children (and that privilege has been extended to disability evaluation), then a family that takes most of the burden off the state for its kids can't be denied the few services they do choose to take advantage of.

Public school advocates often believe, however, that a child's disabilities are most likely to be identified in a classroom, because teachers and staff have some knowledge of or experience with learning and health disabilities and they might spot a problem a parent might miss. This may be true in some cases, but it discounts that parents themselves might be educated and experienced enough to identify issues (a mother with a Masters in nursing is certainly as qualified as the average kindergarten teacher to see a medical problem developing in her child). In addition, the time factor is again a huge one – parents spend intensive time with a child, while teachers and aides do not have the time to deeply interact most days with most students. In fact, splitting a child's time between school and family may mean that neither teachers nor parents pick up on a developing problem, particularly a more subtle one. A child who, for example, has a hearing problem only in the higher ranges may appear to only be a slow learner. Her hearing problem doesn't suggest itself because she seems to be listening and answers questions when addressed directly. Intensive time with the child may uncover the problem.

In any case, the question of whether disabilities and chronic conditions need to be caught early, and in schools, is an open one. Many feel that early "tagging" of students with some conditions can be counterproductive in an institutional setting – boys labeled with an attention deficit might have a hard time crawling out from under the preconceptions that come with the title; a child flagged as having a potential reading disability might simply need a year to become developmentally able to read and may struggle later under an insecurity about her reading because of the unnecessary labeling. Early intervention is not an unadulterated good, either, in an age where long term medication with stimulants and antidepressants has become normal for large numbers of younger and younger children.

Whether a school is the best place for evaluation is also contested. School staff members try to have the best interests of the children at heart, and often they succeed. But it's simply the case that the job of the school is to protect its interests and the interests of its charges in general, not an isolated child's. Often there is no conflict between these goals, but if a student is seen as disrupting a class because of a disability, the evaluation and intervention around that disability might be influenced by the needs of the class, not the student. For example, a child with diabetes might receive intervention in the form of a school nurse who alters the child's blood testing routine to not distract fellow students, rather than following the directives of parents or endocrinologist trying to optimize blood sugar levels for that one kid.

A school may identify and address disabilities well, in any one instance. But many home educating parents believe medical professionals, such as pediatricians and the experts pediatricians refer families to, are the best judges of developing potential issues and the best sources of information on how to work with disability. Home schooling parents often look to doctors, rather than school nurses or counselors, as their primary help in keeping their kids healthy.

Do home school families need to vaccinate? Are they legally required to vaccinate?

Currently state vaccination laws do not require vaccination; they require vaccination in order for a child to attend school. Many states provide ways for families to exempt their children from this requirement in certain cases.

Home students generally, then, do not have to vaccinate as a precondition of schooling. Whether they choose to vaccinate is an entirely different, and more complicated question.

Some outside observers may feel that kids schooling at home can skip vaccines because any outbreaks will probably affect kids grouped in schools, and they will avoid them. However, home schooled kids usually have pretty regular interaction with the public and particularly with peers – dance classes, grocery store visits, church cry rooms, playgrounds all provide exposure risk if any serious outbreaks develop. Home schooling may provide a bit of a time buffer, and even potentially a diminished initial viral load, and that may help students fight disease more effectively – it's hard to say. But it's certain that students schooled at home are still exposed to viruses and bacteria. Home school families have to make their decisions regarding the risks and benefits of vaccination in the same way that traditionally schooling families must.

I hear home school kids get sick more because they aren't exposed to as many germs – the hygiene hypothesis. Is that true?

The "hygiene hypothesis" has been popularized and watered down so much that many folks believe it means it's fortunate if a child is exposed to several serious diseases and scores of smaller ones before the age of two. That would certainly support the case for early child care and preschool, but this is a misreading of the theory.

First, the theory is not about protecting kids from infectious diseases later in life, it is about protecting them from allergies, asthma, and other immune system misfires. The theory is that the body's immune system must be trained in childhood to operate properly, and if it doesn't get on the job training it can turn on the body itself, not recognizing properly the difference between true enemies and normal life. This kind of poor development, according to the theory, comes when antigens are not faced regularly and when "good" bacteria are not acquired from the environment.

This in no way argues that a child must spend four to seven hours every day with two dozen children his own age every weekday of the school year in order to stay healthy. If that were true, autoimmune disease, asthma, and allergies would be on the decline since this kind of situation is normal now, and abnormal in the history of mankind. The rise in incidence of asthma in children is a modern phenomenon, not a problem of, for example, medieval peasant children or pioneer children who interacted with a varied community rather than a homogeneous class.

A child at home who is exposed to colds and bugs from family and friends will naturally develop his immune system, and he will pick up from his biome community the good gut flora and skin bacteria that help his body to stay healthy.

An argument could be made that on-the-ground conditions of home education tend to give a protection to kids there, by way of the hygiene hypothesis. Antimicrobials are often used generously in institutional settings – picture the kindergarteners lined up for their handful of hand sanitizer before snack time. These agents can kill off the good as well as the bad bugs, and leave kids unprotected by their "old friends". Home school families may also tend to be larger, and siblings tend to confer some protection under the hypothesis.

In general, anecdote shows no greater incidence of illness for kids in home school. To suggest home education will make your kids sick is a bit too close to fear mongering to not be considered in the realm of propaganda.

I hear you get sick less if you home school, you aren't exposed to as many germs. Is that true?

Oh, so many home school families wish it were!

You can definitely be more careful about infection if you home school, simply because you have more flexibility. You can avoid communities with a bug and hope you've dodged the bullet. You also have more freedom to pull your kids out of activities when they are sick themselves, and protect others from getting your family illness. But home students get sick, too. In fact, there is a special infection risk in the home school lifestyle in that instead of spending all day in a classroom (where you are likely to get whatever infection is popular at the time), you might spend part of your day at a co-op, part at a library, part in a lesson, and part at a sport – and if there is a different bug passing around at each place, you've been exposed to them all.

Can parents properly serve the nutritional needs of kids without a trained dietician directing the meals through a cafeteria staff and delegating snack policies?

Yes.

Can kids who need physical, occupational, speech or other therapies receive them if they home school?

Certainly.

If a school district provides these therapies for students, the districts are generally required to provide them for home schooled students, also. Funds are generated from taxes paid by all citizens, including home schooling families. Not providing those services, which are targeted for all the state's students, would be like refusing to let someone drive one highway because he chooses not to drive another. Common services aren't generally legally denied just because a family decides to take advantage of only some of them.

However, the family must work with the district to get the therapy in a manner that doesn't put an unreasonable burden on the school therapists. Home school families can't demand therapists come to their home or be available on their schedule. Because of the difficulty with location and scheduling, families sometimes simply use their own health insurance or personal funds to pay private therapists outside the school system.

Is it better for a kid with disabilities to home school?

Generally the answer is that if a child would home school without the disability, he should home school with it. If the child would traditionally school without the disability, he should probably traditionally school with it.

Making a schooling decision based on a medical condition of the child can send a difficult and unintended message to the student. In addition, schools are required to accommodate all students, regardless of disability, and if a school is not serving a student well because of a condition that school is in violation of federal regulation. Public schools cannot see home education as a way to shirk their duty to all our kids.

At the same time, each student's situation is different, and if a student with a disability believes that the benefits particular to home education (flexibility, one on one instruction, individualization, etc.) mean that schooling at home will give him a better quality of life or of education, it's perfectly reasonable to take that into account.

Is it easier to home school a kid with disabilities than to bring him to school?

Again, the answer to this is going to be vastly different for each family, and maybe even from day to day within one family.

There's no doubt that coordinating plans, schedules, accommodations and medical care through a school can be daunting. Most families with a child with a medical condition or a disability have stories of having to fight the system, or deal with an ignorant staff member, or simply struggle to get good attention from staff that may not have the time and resources to comply with care plans. In some ways, it's easier to do complex tasks like medical care yourself rather than through a dozen middlemen.

It's also the case that if a child has a learning disability or a condition that creates special circumstances (e.g. requiring regular absences for doctor visits, etc.), those circumstances can often be better addressed by home schooling because of its flexibility. Material can be presented in ways that accommodate the disability, schedules can be adjusted to school around appointments.

But "easier" is a relative thing. Parents of kids with medical or learning issues can get burned out with care under any circumstances, and being the sole care provider during the day and most of the evening and night as a home school parent can increase the stress. In some ways, it can be "easier" to have a break each school day from care. Other parents might find that continuity of care means not having a "break" actually makes the work easier, in the long run.

There's a kid in my child's class with ADD/ADHD/diabetes/cerebral palsy/Down Syndrome. Shouldn't he be home schooled?

Quite possibly. But not because of the ADD/ADHD/diabetes/cerebral palsy/ Down Syndrome.

Public schools have an obligation to serve all kids, not just the ones easiest to serve. No child can or should be denied the education the government provides through tax revenue because of a medical condition or disability.

Don't kids with disabilities need to go to school to socialize with peers?

No. Home students with disabilities can socialize with peers in the same way home students without disabilities do – through one on one friendships, family social interaction, teams and lessons, and co-ops and church groups.

Schools generally try to integrate disabled students into classrooms today – the original approach was called "mainstreaming" – but schools have in the past tended and sometimes still today are inclined to aggregate disabled children together and isolate them from the general population. Families, on the other hand, naturally include the disabled child in the routines of life, community, friendship. While schools do endeavor to "socialize" the disabled and differently-abled, home education is naturally suited to it.

Does home school make it easier to manage food allergies or Celiac disease?

Yes and no. In a school you have to coordinate with teachers, cafeteria staff, and snack organizers, have plans on record, and be ready for a mistake to lead to an incident.

However, home schooling is, as we've mentioned here already, rarely conducted exclusively at home. Home students generally spend much of many days at cooperatives, in classes, traveling, in the field, or at libraries or museums. All these places can expose kids to allergens and triggers, and parents have little control over and sometimes little access to knowledge about these venues.

Celiac and allergies are simply difficult burdens to struggle under, no matter your environment. Most families manage it quite well.

Can home school kids play team sports?

Of course. Municipal leagues, camps and clubs, parks and recreation departments, and private competitive teams are all options for home students.

In most states, students also are legally protected if they choose to play a team sport through their local public school. Again, public schools are maintained for the use of all school-aged residents, choosing not to use one product of the schools shouldn't disqualify those residents from using other ones. Home schoolers do, however, have to participate in ways that don't create extra work for the schools or give unfair competitive advantage to one school over another.

Private schools also sometimes allow home students to join their teams and compete, and law can protect that, also.

What are the health advantages of home schooling for a typical child?

Most of the advantages are going to come from the two home school benefits mentioned already repeatedly – time and flexibility.

Students who choose to be active will find that the increased efficiency of home education gives them more time to pursue their nonacademic interests. They will be able to optimize the timing of their activities – for example, hike during prime daylight hours – by shifting schoolwork out of those select time spots.

Nutrition also is often higher quality at home, where scratch cooking can replace processed cafeteria meals.

Not all families will take full advantage of these opportunities, but they are available to those who want them.

Do you have P.E. in home school?

Some cooperatives offer physical education classes, or variations on them, such as soccer instruction or outside games for kindergarteners.

It's rare for a home education physical education program to mimic a school program. What parents normally do is incorporate an active lifestyle and sports into their day. Many home school families spend substantial hours in outdoor recreation – hiking, hunting, fishing, camping, boating. Others have children who compete in gymnastics or swimming or track, or who study dance. A home program can make it easier to select childhood activities that can be seamlessly continued into young adulthood and adulthood, setting up habits for life.

Support Materials

The internet age makes it easy to find materials with which to supplement education programs; you can bring an incredible amount of information into the home and never need to worry about a shortage of materials if you have a connection, and possibly a printer. With over 1.5 million home educated students in America, small innovators as well as large corporations are coming to understand there is a market for packaged materials and assistance in instruction.

Most mid-sized towns also have at least one teacher supply store. These outlets are stocked with maps, globes, charts, posters, workbooks, worksheet collections, unit study packages, small lab kits, educational games and toys. They are happy to sell to home school families.

What are some support sites for penmanship instruction?

There's nothing wrong with picking up a generic writing handbook, or one of the large pads with dashed division lines, for writing practice. Many families have students simply practice copy work each day (from, for example, a Bible verse or a poem), or take dictation; others work a system starting with the alphabet in print and moving to phrases and quotes in script.

Zaner-Bloser is the go-to site for handwriting resources, it's a system that has been used by schools for decades and much of it is accessible online.

What is NaNoWriMo?

National Novel Writing Month is a movement to motivate fiction writers. The goal is to finish a rough manuscript for a novel during the month of November, and the Web site and community support this goal. This is an adult project, but the team has added a teen section to its site. While an excellent source, parental supervision is suggested.

What kind of local societies can be used to supplement education programs?

  Bunches of them.

  Astronomical societies often have open lectures or telescope viewing nights. Running clubs sometimes welcome families or older students. Parks and recreation departments and cooperative extension sponsored 4H clubs can be useful. Geology clubs can supplement an earth science course with lectures, shows, and field trips. The Audubon Society also hosts field trips, sometimes for families. Zoos and museums often have reciprocal agreements with institutions across the country so that membership in one means a family can visit dozens over the years. Libraries are, of course, great book and research material repositories but are increasingly offering courses, lectures, and clubs, often oriented to home educators – for example, there might be a science lab at one library, a French club at another. Quilting and craft societies can pass on skills and often are involved in charitable activities. National and state parks have full calendars of lectures, hikes, and other events, and programs like the National Parks' Junior Ranger Program provide goals and incentives – patches, pins, or other tokens. Parks, libraries, clubs, hospitals, and local churches and charities often offer volunteer opportunities.

How can home school families take advantage of colleges and universities in the area?

Home students in some states are able, in high school, to use concurrent education programs to use public school money to attend local colleges and count the credits towards both their high school and their college transcripts.

More informally, colleges often have open lectures or music, art, and theater exhibitions.

What are some supplemental fun programs for math?

There are many, many online math programs, such as the Sketch's World games that can be selected for any of the four arithmetic operations. Some book resources include the British *Murderous Maths* series, which twists through a plot line involving math; *Family Math*, a book with dozens of games that can be played at different levels to reinforce math sense; and Dover Publications' line of math game and puzzle books.

The *Life of Fred* series from Polka Dot Press has become immensely popular in recent years. The Fred books are designed to teach math using a narrative. They are used independently by students; there are small sections of practice problems they check themselves with each story chapter. After a number of sections the students must pass a "bridge" in order to continue reading the story. Students who do not pass the bridge must review and try the next bridge – they get five attempts. The series now takes students from early years all the way through college math, and the author has added other subjects to his list.

What are some sources of Internet information not directly connected with institutional schools?

Parents usually find sources of information that are consistently useful for them. Some use the National Geographic site or magazines, the NASA site, YouTube (with filters and supervision) and schooltube, and the various educational series' by Brady Haran.

How can supply companies help a home school educator build a science program?

There are companies like Home Science Tools that sell lab supplies for home school families, and ones like Carolina Biological Company and Quality Science Labs that sell to schools and homes. You can buy live items (like frogs or algae) chemistry supplies, and dissection kits. Most experiments that can be done in a high school laboratory can be done at home with safety protocols and supplies from these companies. Many of the science curriculum sets also have optional lab kits you can purchase.

Is it appropriate for home school students to learn through videos?

Some families prefer to keep video learning entirely off the plate, but others use series' such as *The Way Things Work* and *Maths Challenge* to supplement their math, *Muzzy* to start kids on a foreign language, and DK or NOVA programs as extras when teaching science. The Great Courses company provides audio and video from college lecturers on scores on subjects. Many of these video resources are available through libraries.

What's the deal with Usborne and DK?

These publishers don't specifically publish for home school families, but their comprehensive libraries of lively educational references are invaluable. Their science, geography, math, foreign language, and history books are terrific to use as a skeleton or as a supplement, accessible to student readers, and well illustrated. They are also widely available in library nonfiction sections.

How is Cathy Duffy's site helpful?

Cathy Duffy runs a review site for materials and curricula. Her site is a great starting place for new home educators.

What is the Khan Academy craze about?

Salman Khan began his unexpected rise to fame when he posted a number of explanatory math videos on YouTube for his cousin and friends. The videos began to be used by students across the states, eventually even gathering an overseas following.

The series is useful for traditional students looking for extra help outside of school, but many home school parents learned they could build some of their math programs around his explanations.

Khan has since expanded his endeavor, bringing in other contributors and trying to innovate a new way of learning.

Is there a site that aggregates curricula for download?

CurrClick is a growing site that manages independent sellers' interactions with buyers. Their offerings are video courses and downloadable units on a range of topics. Many of the sellers are amateur experts, and a ratings system helps buyers determine the quality of the material. In some ways, CurrClick is like the Etsy of curricula.

Post-Secondary

One of the most frequent questions about home school – probably up in the top three with "How are you going to teach calculus or other advanced subjects?" and the dreaded "What about socialization?", is whether a home school student can still go to college. We've been pretty thoroughly trained to believe that the credential – the stamped paper with "graduated" on it – is essential to advancement. In reality, more and more colleges and universities are recognizing that qualifications are what matter, not credentials.

Of course, universities still have to find a way to evaluate an applicant's qualifications. Fortunately, most are well versed in that at this point.

Do home schooled students go to college?

They do. In fact, according to a 2009 University of St. Thomas study referenced in *U.S. News & World Report*, they seem to graduate college at a higher rate than those traditionally schooled (with graduation from college being a better marker of success than initial attendance), and grade higher while they are there.

Our family has always gone to Loyalty University, it's a long tradition. Will they take my home schooled grandchildren?

Very probably. Why not ask them?

If one university choice (or any other post-secondary path) is particularly important to a family, it's a good idea to contact that university during the early high school years to make sure you orient your program and your record keeping in a way that maximizes your appeal to that university. The school may want a traditional transcript (which the parent can create) or be happy to depend on test scores (which the parent can then prioritize).

Home students are accepted by most universities and colleges now, including the military academies and the Ivy League schools. Some institutions even seek them out. A little research ahead of time is the best way to make sure you match their application preferences to a "T".

What is the admissions process for home schooled kids, do you need a transcript, letters of recommendation, and a diploma?

This varies by school. It's best to check the school's Web site or call or write the admissions office and find their preferences. Some won't give two figs about a paper diploma but need a formal transcript with a description of classes taken and a grade. Others might put a lot of weight on the recommendation of folks that know the student's qualifications.

In your investigation, try to ferret out not just what the university's basic requirements are, but which records the university seems to value highest.

Will the best universities accept home schooled applicants?

While this question's answer depends a bit on what the meaning of "best" is, if the conventional meaning is taken this answer is indisputably "yes".

Some universities are tolerant of home education, some are welcoming, and some are eager to encourage home students' application.

If you read the guidelines for Stanford admission, for example, there is a distinct whiff of suspicion. A student will need to explain why he is home educated, and will have to find a way to fully prove his qualifications, which will need to be very high, as all Stanford applicants' qualifications should be. Some of the more politically left oriented universities are likely to still suspect a home student as being an indoctrinated conservative Christian, so that hurdle will have to be jumped. With that said, Stanford accepted in 2012 27% of home schooled applicants, and only 5% of traditionally schooled applicants.

The Air Force and Naval academies welcome home students, but because their decision process includes a "leadership" evaluation, both note that a substitute for a school sports program will strengthen an application. Home students can, of course, normally participate in public school sports, so that choice might be made by someone aiming for an academy.

Notre Dame's Web site features a link to a 2013 Mark Snyder study that tentatively suggests that students in private Catholic colleges who were home educated perform better than both public schooled students and parochial schooled students. Notre Dame is friendly to home study but suggests home educated students use standardized test scores to demonstrate their academic qualifications.

Columbia's admissions page explicitly places home students on the same footing with the traditionally schooled – all applications will be evaluated in the same manner.

MIT's admissions page states, "MIT has a long history of admitting homeschooled students, and these students are successful and vibrant members of our community. . . One quality that we look for in all of our applicants is evidence of having taken initiative, showing an entrepreneurial spirit, taking full advantage of opportunities. Many of our admitted homeschooled applicants have really shined in this area."

The opinion of some home education pundits, such as Penelope Trunk, is that at the higher levels of admissions competition it is getting harder and harder for students to differentiate themselves from other applicants – Trunk contends home education can be a "hook" that catches the attention of admissions officers, particularly in the "best" schools.

Do you have to get a GED to move on to college? Does it help?

Students who graduate from a home program don't need a GED to apply to college any more than students who graduate from traditional programs do.

Whether a GED helps on applications is a bit of an open question. Some parents feel it is a good way to reassure colleges that the student is just as "done" with high school as a student with a paper diploma from a school district is. This seems reasonable, but in an environment where home education is normally understood by admissions offices and where the GED is still often seen as (likely unfairly) the choice for those who drop out of high school, having a GED may work against a student.

Again, the best way to decide whether to complete one or not is to contact the colleges you have an interest in and ask how it would be viewed by their admissions counselors.

Will the military accept kids who didn't graduate from a public or private school institution? Will the academies accept them, and ROTC programs?

Home graduates can enlist in all the services and apply for ROTC scholarships or to the military academies. Very careful attention to the specific application requirements and recommendations is suggested.

Signing bonuses are often based on education level, so home students need to precisely document their achievement of graduation if they intend to enlist.

What is concurrent education?

Students from all schooling methods can use concurrent education, but it can be a particularly handy tool for home students because it can help provide records of completion for high school students.

Concurrent education is completed through any of the many programs in different states where a high school student is able to take a state college course (often through a community college) and "count" that on both her high school transcript and as a college credit. Districts sometimes will pay the tuition for the college course. In this way, a student can get general education credits for early in his college career or begin a vocational program or associates degree before finishing high school.

Home students can use concurrent, or dual credit, education to fill out a transcript. This can be handy for the family but also can be useful for proving credentials for college applications. Concurrent education also means home students can save a year or more's college tuition, if they are college bound and attend a school that takes the transferred credits.

What is a MOOC, and why would I want my niece to have anything to do with one?

MOOC stands for Massive Open Online Course. Students of all kinds can visit a MOOC site and select from courses, often taught by professors at solid universities and colleges, and study that coursework online. There are different formats that are used, but generally a student registers with the site, selects the course or courses, and logs in to get assignments and watch or listen to lectures. There is sometimes a discussion forum or other interactive features. The course might be conducted in real time or archived and available on the student's schedule.

There are sometimes ways to gain credentials for taking a MOOC – usually a certificate. It is not a traditional course in that a student submits assignments and tests that are evaluated in order to assign a grade – tests, quizzes, and work are sometimes automatically graded online, the feedback is more automated, the student will not usually be able to use the course as a graded transcript item. But certificates from coursework can be listed as a kind of extracurricular activity.

Those interested in MOOCs often use Coursera or edX, or sites associated with specific universities such as Harvard, Yale, or Hillsdale.

MOOCs aren't the only form of online learning. Most colleges and universities offer distance education now. A student with a strong interest may be able to enroll in a full online course from a post-secondary school of her choice and receive a complete grade and college credit. This method is often expensive, however. MOOCs are generally free.

What is a CLEP, and what use could my nephew possibly have for it?

The College Level Examination Program is administered by the College Board, the same folks that provide AP and SAT testing.

CLEP testing is a way to sometimes earn college credits by "testing out" of basic general classes. An American literature CLEP test, for example, evaluates whether a student has the knowledge and understanding of the subject that he would be expected to have achieved after taking two semesters of college American literature. Students in college can then work independently on these core subject and save money by taking a test instead of a course.

High school students can also study and take CLEP exams. It can be a highly economically efficient way to shorten a college career, and can be incorporated into a home program – the home educating parent simply teaches high school subjects she would have taught anyway at an advanced level, and then uses the CLEP as a kind of final exam.

It needs to be noted that acceptance of a CLEP pass as a transfer credit depends upon the school the student will be attending. Some universities accept CLEP results, some don't, and some accept them only with conditions.

Home school programs can also take advantage of AP (Advanced Placement) testing to advance past some general college courses.

Socialization

Probably the greatest concern extended family and friends have when they learn a child will be educated at home is whether he will become a well rounded, psychologically stable adult who is able to interact well with others. This isn't really a new topic; ever since the days when "plays well with others" was an encouraging note on elementary school report cards we've looked to school professionals to tell us whether our kids were or weren't developing the ability to form healthy relationships. As frustrated as home educating parents can become at the question, most would acknowledge that they pay special attention to making sure the social needs of their children are met. In this way, home schooled kids often wind up in the old position of having to be "twice as good to be considered half as good", and so may in the end be pushed as a population to a standard of excellence not experienced in institutionally schooled children. If a shy child or a rambunctious child is, for example, acting awkwardly at a birthday party, the behavior will only be attributed to educational choice if the kid is home schooled. You'll rarely hear gossiping adults whisper, "Look at little Harry, he can't seem to talk with the other boys," and then shake their heads and add, "He's public schooled, you know."

Do home schooled kids go to dances?

If they want to. Normally, they do want to.

Home schooled students often are friends with kids in public or private schools, and are invited to attend as dates.

Home school community groups normally organize dances and other types of social events several times a year.

Those dances may look a bit different from public school dances (or they may not), depending on the culture of the local home school community. Sometimes dances are multi-aged, or whole family. If the home school community is highly religious, the tenor of the night will usually reflect religious values to one degree or another. The dance will likely be held at a community center, church communal space, or rented space.

But the rest is normally about the same.

Do home schooled kids date?

If they choose to, and if they are permitted to date by their parents – just like traditionally schooled kids. Because home education today is often a choice made by cultural conservatives, this may be reflected in the way the kids date or the age at which they date. However, home school itself doesn't dictate dating rules.

Do home school families try to control who their kids can be friends with?

Again, this is nothing particular to home education. Many parents feel, justly or unjustly, that they should have some degree of influence over their children's social choices.

Counter-intuitively, sometimes children who are home educated find that they are more free of parental controls in their friendships than they would be if they were institutionally schooled. Parents who select private schools for their children often do so in part in order to narrow the peer group for their kids – either to encourage their kids to hang out with kids of the same religious perspective or with kids whose families value education similarly, or with kids from, frankly, a similar socio-economic group. Within public schools there are often "gifted" programs or other methods of grouping kids that parents can harness to limit the kinds of peers their students are exposed to. The nature of American schooling – neighborhood and district based – usually means that kids who are in public school will normally attend school with students of a similar class and often even racial background.

Home education, however, is equally open to families of all classes, belief systems, races, cultural backgrounds, and educational abilities. It is true that the nature of home education means the very poor or uneducated cannot as often easily access it – but with work, it is possible. Home school communities sometimes are fairly homogeneous, but in other places they may be an atypically diverse educational environment. Parents who want to use a certain kind of school to limit who their kids can be friends with often won't find home education very useful in this regard.

In addition, parents with kids in traditional schools sometimes feel they need to impose controls on their kids' friendships because they do not want them to have friends who will be "bad influences". The students are at school with their peers, with a low ratio of adults to young people, for 35 to 50 hours every week. It is hard to address problems as they come up, in that situation. But socialization in home education is normally done in the same building as siblings and parents – bad acts will be noticed and addressed more often in real time. The parents have the opportunity to address the problems and allow relationships to continue, rather than feeling they need to end relationships in order to avoid problems.

Do parents who home school not want their kids to have peer relationships at all? Do they only want their kids to be friends with their siblings?

Having a good relationship with family doesn't preclude having a good relationship with peers. In fact, there is a body of thinking that suggests the best way for a young person to develop into a relationally healthy adult is to learn how to navigate the messy world of human interdependence within the family, and then to take those social skills and practice them in the world of peers, friends, and acquaintances. If children learn how to socialize from adults (normally family), they will then be able to apply that knowledge well with their peers. But if they learn how to socialize from each other (as they do in same-aged classrooms), they are likely to learn poorly and have a hard time correcting that bad instruction as the years go on and they continue to be expected to learn from each other. Teens learning from other teens how to behave with each other is a recipe for the kind of social dysfunction some sectors of our society are seeing today.

Gordon Neufeld's excellent book, *Hold On To Your Kids*, makes the case that peer orientation leads to poor social development and insecure young people. When adolescents, for example, depend upon each other to develop their social skills and self respect, they are relying upon naturally emotionally fragile people just when they are naturally most emotionally fragile themselves. Young people need to have a healthy social balance established within themselves already, from family and community, before venturing out to build relationships with the developing humans of their peer group.

So home schooling parents very much want their kids to have peer relationships. They simply want them to have strong, healthy, moral, and long standing ones rather than insecure, damaging, unhealthy, unsavory, and fleeting ones.

Why do some home school parents not like institutional school socialization practices, are they against socialization?

While not universal, the standard school approach to social development is to throw 20 to 30 kids of the same age into a classroom together for many hours each day, give them occasional general lessons about good and bad behavior, and then try to address any bad social behavior that occurs with discipline and programs that discourage bullying, drug use, and teen pregnancy.

Home educators find this to be sub-optimal, and as they do not have to teach large numbers of kids they have no personal relationship with at one time, they can use other methods to encourage social development. They aren't against socialization, but they do not take the same approach to socialization that schools normally do.

Is there a difference between socialization and socializing?

Certainly. Socialization is a process of learning how to relate to other human beings. It is complex and ongoing, and good models aid in success.

Socializing is what you do when the teacher isn't looking.

Then how do home school families accomplish socialization?

Home school socialization is varied. There are many opportunities for learning good relational skills, and any one family may use one or more. There are formal opportunities, like cooperative classes or group tutoring sessions. There are event such as dances, potlucks, religious gatherings, field trips and travel. There are internships, jobs, and volunteer work. But much social interaction is very informal – families simply get together, either as whole families, as individuals visiting and chatting, or both. Phone conversations, electronic messaging, and Skype and Facetime all have their place, especially among female teens.

Can you home school properly if you only have one child?

Yes, you certainly can. Every family is different and every family configuration triggers its own particular insecurities, but "only" children can certainly do very well in home education. Any parent with concerns on this account should contact a local home school group and ask if a family which also has one child can talk to them about their home school choice.

When large families home school, do the kids have a hard time acting their age?

Not at all. But sometimes they have the luxury of acting other ages, also.

As a general rule, children in large home school families can show early maturity in many areas. They tend to acquire responsibilities, both towards their siblings and towards their own education. A degree of self-sufficiency is usually required, as is, paradoxically, a degree of communal cooperation.

An older teen schooling at home is likely to be able to run part of the household, take on some of the education for younger siblings or even for home school groups of younger students, potentially integrate into a family business, while at the same time planning and preparing for her own individual future path.

Being around a range of younger kids, however, gives older students the freedom to keep open to play and fun. An adolescent who can both help with family bookkeeping and play soldier with his younger siblings has an emotional, developmental, and creative range that serves him in many ways.

If, then, you see a home student who is working behind the counter at a family business, don't assume he has been expected to leave his childhood behind; and if you see a teen playing doll tea party with a group of littles, understand she's comfortable enough in her own maturity to be able to sit on the floor with her sister and sister's friends.

I talked to a home schooled kid the other day, he was very shy/ quiet/ spacey/ hysterical/ goofy/ awkward/ aggressive/ passive/ verbal/ nonverbal. Is that about lack of socialization?

Would you ask the same if the child weren't home educated? Have you never seen those traits in traditionally schooled children?

Sometimes, as adults, we tend to put on the rose-colored glasses when looking back at our school days (although at other times we see them in an overly harsh glare). A half hour spent with a niece or grandchild at a public playground can give us some perspective on child socialization. Most children go through a shy phase, a hysterical phase, or both; most have aggressive days and passive days. Kids develop their personalities over time and the world is a complicated place, it's good if we all remember to give kids from public, private, and home schools all a bit of a break.

If a child seems to have a long standing social difficulty that is becoming calcified as personality, it's good to first check our preconceptions – is that a problem, or is it just a difference? If, then, it seems to be a problem, there may be organic causes which can be nutritionally or medically addressed, or a problem with the social environment that needs to be identified. A home student is just as likely to have social awkwardness due to environment as an institutionally schooled child is. The advantage for the home student is that the environment can be adjusted, while the traditionally schooled student is fairly stuck with his situation – although many parents try a transfer from a classroom or a teacher, a change in grade level, or even a switch to another school when they feel it's necessary.

I saw a home school kid interacting with regular kids the other day, she didn't fit in. Won't this kind of thing be a problem for her all her life?

Is the home schooled kid, then, "irregular"?

This is a situation home schooling parents need to deal with at times. Home educated students are likely to be a bit different from students at Jones High School, and when you have a mixed group (e.g. for a competition, performance, seminar, testing, etc.), a home student among Jones HS students is likely to not fit perfectly at first.

But it is also the case that Smith High School students will be a bit different in their tastes and experiences from Jones High School students, and one SHS student in a crowd of JHS students will similarly take some time to find her sea legs.

Home students often participate in events and activities with schools, but traditionally schooled students rarely seek out home school events to join (although it does happen, and they are generally welcome). If you see a home student seeming a bit like the odd man out, it's probably because she has been thrown into unfamiliar territory, and she is working it out. Home students become adept at sorting out how to navigate unfamiliar territory; this gives them skills they will use their entire lives.

Is it all right to ask a kid about her home school program?

Certainly, just in the way you would ask about a kid's day or year at school. It is inappropriate to *grill* a child about her schooling, though, in either case.

It is always tempting to play "pop quiz" with a student, either as a conversation starter or to buffer your confidence that the child is being well educated. This is something adults do no matter how a child is schooled. But it is especially challenging when a child is home educated, because if Aunt Sue or Neighbor Bill pops the quiz and determines the traditionally schooled student is being poorly taught, the student does not feel her family is under scrutiny or attack.

There are also some curious adults with biases against home education, usually based on lack of experience, who play "gotcha" with their quizzing. You may not be one of these, but if you start gently questioning a student you may get stonewalled if the kid has run into this sort of thing before.

Some well-intentioned adults play quiz games because they are trying to give home students the opportunity to show how brilliant they are. This can backfire; if the kid doesn't know the answer to a softball question, everyone is uncomfortable. If she knows it, she has likely been trained against showing off and she'll feel uncomfortable answering.

The best way to discuss home school is to ask open ended questions at first, and more specific ones later. Rather than jumping in with, "Are you able to play on a baseball team?", ask, "What's your favorite outside activity?" Instead of asking what level math a student is studying, ask what one of his last math lessons talked about, or what his favorite subject is.

It's also helpful to telegraph that you are not confused by or aggravated by atypical answers. For example, home students often are asked the standard "what grade are you in" question. That's not a hard one to answer – I'm in fourth grade for English, but fifth grade for math and third for most everything else. But when students answer this way, they learn it can flummox and irritate the questioner, so the whole exchange becomes unhappy. Listen to the answers as they come, instead of expecting one answer and being thrown off when you get something else, and you'll ease the conversation.

Home school should not be an avoided topic, but also doesn't need to be the first topic out of the gate. Because for decades most young Americans have attended school, asking about school tends to be a "safe" ask when you meet a student and don't know what else to say – kind of like "So, what work do you do?" is the standard question for an adult you've just met. It's handy in any instance, though, to have a raft of conversation starters – you can ask about interests, experiences, family and friends, pets and favorites. Launching into the stereotypical "What grade are you in, what's your favorite subject, do you like school" line of questioning gets weary for all kids, not just home schooled ones.

Support Organizations

There are a number of niches support organizations fill for home education. Some are nonprofits that help with legal, technical, academic, or elective topics. Others are general support organizations that serve young people and that have diversified and specialized to give particular support for the growing number of home schooled families.

How do home school families use public libraries?

Often extensively.

Many home school families are fairly voracious in their consumption of books. Particularly when using a living or great books program, buying one to five books a week per child can become very expensive very quickly. It's usually easy to identify a home school family at the library – they're there in the middle of a school day – but a second clue is if each child is carrying a roomy and sturdy bag for books. Some even use small suitcases.

Libraries today, though, have become additionally useful with new programs that fit well with home education. Most have a request and hold system, so that a parent or student can "order" books online and pick them up at the library he uses. This is a fabulous time saver, and since many libraries have agreements to share materials across their states, sometimes even with college and university libraries, library users now have access to an unprecedented wealth of material.

Ebook access is also a handy feature of the modern library. Home students with readers can check out electronically formatted books from their homes.

Many libraries are also coming to understand their unique role with the home school community, and are actively catering to the population with classes and resource sharing. For example, some have set up language labs so that students can use online foreign language resources, and couple that with real world language meetings. Some make their facilities available for home school writing or science groups. The interaction between library staff and home school communities can still be a little awkward – home education remains imperfectly understood. But the potential for symbiotic growth is high. As libraries work to find new ways to be useful in an internet age, their importance to folks of all ages and in all sectors who are independently educating can't be overlooked.

Are there online forums that support the parents?

Yes. The resource section of this booklet will list some sites, but generally you will find them associated with a particular home school method or with a group or association. The Well Trained Mind forum, for example, is extensive and helpful.

Are there online forums that support the kids?

Security issues make forums for children online more difficult. Some programs that home students use – such as game or writing sites –

certainly have forums, boards, etc. and students may identify themselves as home schooled and receive support that way.

What is CHEC? Home Schoolers of Maine? SCHEA? ENOCH?

Every state has home school organizations that are set up to support and guide families in their work. *Practical Homeschooling Magazine* has a thorough list of state organizations on its Web site. State groups are handy because home education regulation varies from state to state. Most local areas also have community groups of one sort or another, if only Internet groups. Churches sometimes also have local home school groups associated with them.

Can home schoolers participate in math and science competitions and fairs, spelling and geography bees, etc.?

Yes.

Most of the major competitive organizations now accommodate home education. For example, Science Olympiad and the Scripps National Spelling Bee both make it easy for home school students to compete. Often home school families do need to create a local group in order to best enter.

What is the major support organization for home school law?

The Home School Legal Defense Association (HSLDA) is the most aggressive and extensive legal support organization out there. HSLDA is definitively an advocacy group, and as such it isn't everyone's cup of tea; but the good work they have done to promote freedom to school in state legislatures and in defending members (and even nonmembers) from assaults on their rights by the ignorant is undeniable.

What is an umbrella school? Do all families use them?

Umbrella schools provide logistics help for home school families. They keep track of state law and compliance, record-keeping, testing updates, and sometimes help with transcripts. In general, they do the paperwork for you. Just like a small business owner may feel very competent in his field but hire a bookkeeper to do accounts, a home school parent may feel very comfortable with the schooling but less so with the red tape and filing. Umbrella schools fill that niche.

They are an option for use, but in no way required. Most families don't take advantage of their services, but many do.

What are online home school programs?

Online schools like Mother of Divine Grace are programs that will deliver an entire school package over the Internet. Most of the work in these programs is the responsibility of (often older) students, who are supported by online teachers and staff. Parents facilitate the teaching. Materials and tests are submitted to the online school for evaluation.

These programs can be expensive, but many families find they bring order, rigor, and independence to their home program. Good internet access and computer skills are necessary. Students sometimes can use these programs part time rather than sign up for the full raft of classes.

What is a co-op?

Home school cooperatives come in many shapes and sizes. In some locations, co-ops are more akin to businesses. Teachers are hired or come together cooperatively and present classes for students, who pay for the instruction.

In other places, parents themselves organize to teach groups including their own and other families.

Co-ops can meet for a half or a full day, one or more times a week.

Why?

Why do families home school? Usually we expect a political or religious answer, and sometimes we receive it. But there are a great number of reasons to home school and any one family usually has more than one. It's a hard decision, declining public education, and one that involves a great deal of work and sacrifice. Families don't make that call lightly.

Do some parents home school because they were home schooled themselves?

We have now, interestingly, entered an age where there are a significant number of second-generation home school families. This brings a unique perspective to the community at large. Most parents who choose to school at home were schooled in institutions, private or public, themselves; it's often hard to shake the preconceptions that come with that background. Second generation home educated families don't harbor those preconceptions, and can come to the endeavor from a more organic perspective.

This is still, however, a fairly rare phenomenon. Consider, also, that a man or woman who is home educated will not necessarily make the same choice for his or her own children.

Do parents home school to avoid peer problems, like bullying?

This is a difficult and tense question.

The public perception often is that home school is a way to "escape" a difficult specific situation in a school.

This is undoubtedly the case for some. A student with a difficult personal situation may find that a trigger to look into home education, and that student may find, once she is home educating, that the lifestyle fits her well.

139

The accusation, though, is that home school is used as a way to "run away" from the "real world" rather than "learn to deal" with difficult situations.

It is rare for a family to home school long-term based on one incident. It is probably the case that some students who have problems with relationships, bullying, teacher conflicts, or discipline or drug issues at school spend some time out of the school, and they may do some school work at home, and may even label themselves "home schooled". Home schooling in these cases, though, is not an actual choice but more of a temporary fall back. These families are not committed to home education (why would they be, when they are not choosing for it but falling into it as a stop gap safety net?) and they are usually not truly interested in the life changes needed to make the home education program work. When they return to traditional schooling, they often have actually had an educational gap rather than a trial of home education.

Sure, but be honest, don't families home school sometimes because they don't like the atmosphere of schools?

Yes – yes, they do.

Many modern American parents find portions of the social atmosphere of institutional schooling problematic. There are many ways to deal with this.

Each family and situation will be different. But parents who stick with traditional schooling need to understand that home educators aren't trying to take an "easy" road for their kids – all kids must face adversity, all must deal with relationships and with misbehavior directed at themselves, all must stand up to bullying or "mean girls", all must at some point build in themselves the ability to "cope" with the sordid side of human interaction. Home educating families feel, though, that living in a healthy environment equips their kids to deal with the occasional interaction with dysfunction; some have found their schools to be dysfunctional, and feel that living in a dysfunctional environment inhibits the development of the mental and emotional health needed to "deal with" social situations correctly – that it can instead create a siege mentality, habits of collaboration , or an inclination to create personas. Home students don't run away from the messy world of human relationships, they maximize the health of their daily relationships in order to better face unhealthy situations when they occur.

But my school was pretty awful, and I survived.

That's sincerely a good thing, survival. We live, however, in one of the most blessed times and places in the history of man. We might strive for more for our children than survival.

We also have an obligation to raise children in a healthy manner, because we live in a time where humans are immensely powerful and our choices as civilized beings have intense and expansive impacts. The president who chooses whether to go to war, the doctor who chooses whether and how to treat a patient, the voter who decides how to approach issues of justice, the worker who gets up each day and determines whether it's important to give an honest day's work for an honest day's pay, the employer who must determine how to view and treat his employees – it's good for all these people to be mentally and emotionally healthy. Our early citizens were not institutionally educated, if the relatively new practice of institutional education leads to social dysfunction over the generations, our national culture will suffer.

In addition, the definition of "awful" has changed in the last few decades. In the past, students have faced severe trials, but in many instances they were of a very different nature. This doesn't discount the severity – a black student attending a largely white elementary school in 1969 certainly had no easy life. But that same black student in 2010 might, in her fully integrated elementary school, face sexual aggressiveness or assault. She may also still face a racism that is no doubt less immediately threatening but just as dispiriting and oppressive. A student in a 1954 urban high school might carry scars from fights. A student in many 2010 urban high schools might leave 12 years of schooling without being able to read, working for the drug dealers that ruled his school. A student in a rural junior high in 1970 undoubtedly knew several of his classmates who had early pregnancies, abortions, or drug problems. A student in a rural 2010 middle school knows well that nearly half of his peers are sexually active, and he's living in a world where syphilis and gonorrhea are treatable but again on the rise and there are 50,000 new cases of HIV in the U.S. each year.

The world is not necessarily harder, but it is different, and before judging whether a kid needs to be in a school to "toughen up", an outsider needs to really get to know that school and whether its culture is likely to toughen or break down a young person.

I heard about a kid who was home schooled so she could play the violin more. That can't be right, can it?

Oh, it can.

Some kids home school as an adjunct to another choice – to pursue a special skill or interest. A young person with a drive to excel in one area will find that the efficiency of home education gives her more time to endeavor in that specialized field.

This is a choice that should not be made lightly, of course, because rearranging an entire educational life based on one interest is not always a good plan. But sometimes it turns out exceptionally well. Even if the particular endeavor (a sport, a performance art, a career interest) eventually becomes less important, the child has learned self-direction, discipline, and sacrifice.

Are some kids home schooled because they've been expelled?

Expelled children are still required to be educated, so sometimes they are given home programs with teacher visits or guidance so they can continue the school's program but in their own homes. Because this is still directed by the traditional school, many find it only slightly related to actual home education. But it does take place in the home.

Certainly a few students have found their way to committed, independent home education after an expulsion, either because the expulsion was unjust and this soured the family on traditional schooling, or because a repentance followed the expulsion and the family decided to move to home education for other reasons after seeing the benefits of leaving traditional schools.

Do some leave school after a trauma?

Public education is a product all Americans have free access to. The point of compulsory universal education is to educate all students, not just the ones easiest to educate, for the benefit of the nation, not the individual student. Students who have had a difficult experience in school are encouraged to stay in the system, and have the legal right to do so no matter what reasonable accommodations the school has to provide to make that possible.

Some families may choose to leave school after a trauma if the school environment inherently worsens the situation or if the school was complicit in the trauma. Although these students have the right to continue in the school, they may feel the school has, by the poor choices or behavior of its staff, lost the right to retain them as students.

Are home schooled kids sheltered?

They can be. So can traditionally schooled kids. Individual parents all choose different ways in which to raise their children. Some feel a wide range of exposure to positive and negative influences is important; some feel young people should have encouraging and nutritious experiences as much as possible, and be exposed to unhealthy aspects of life only as necessary. Both these kinds of parents are found in home and institutional education.

Both kinds of parents are more likely to succeed in their efforts, though, in home education. The parent who wishes to limit unhealthy influences will find she cannot limit them while her children are in the care of peers. The parent who wishes her child to have a wide range of experiences will find that the institutional school narrowly limits her child's opportunity for those – in home education, the parent can bring the student into wildly heterogeneous environments, but the school classroom will necessarily be fairly homogeneous.

In the end, home schooling allows a parent to have more say in how a child is raised, because he has more time with his child. How the parent chooses to exercise that say is unique to each parent.

Do Christian home schooled girls only learn to cook and sew?

Nope. You've been watching too much reality TV. They sometimes learn to cook and sew in addition to learning academic subjects. Only on cable and satellite can teaching your child extra subjects be painted as keeping her ignorant.

How does home school fit with travel?

A family fond of travel and that has the economic ability to do so (e.g. telecommutes for work or works in the field, earns enough to travel safely) can build an entire curriculum out of travel; some take a year and visit every state in an RV, for instance, schooling on the road. "Car schooling" is practiced to some degree even by families who don't travel so extensively – a day trip midweek can be a great hands on experience, and math can be done from the back seat as easily as from the kitchen table (carsickness being a limiting factor, of course).

How does home school help with family time for families with unusual schedules?

For families where one or both parents work weekends, nights, or on a "two weeks gone, one week home" sort of schedule, home schooling can be of great benefit. Students can work while the parent is working and spend time with family when it is available, instead of missing dad or mom's only day off because it's a Tuesday.

Do parents home school because of school shootings? Isn't that an overreaction?

Parents sometimes home school because we now have a school culture that makes school shootings possible. While all parents are concerned about the danger of any one incident, most are aware that statistically a child is much more likely to get hurt traveling back and forth to school each day than in a shooting incident.

Do liberal home schoolers teach their girls to be radical feminists?

I'm sure there's one out there somewhere, and she'll probably have her own TV show soon. But generally no, liberal and conservative home school parents want their children to grow up with values and recognize that educating them at home might be a straightforward way to help that happen. Obviously, there are common values and then there are values that liberals will be more friendly towards (and teach their children more diligently) and values that conservatives will be more friendly towards (and teach their children more diligently). But a parent is rarely willing to take the hit on finances, time, patience, and life-span that home schooling brings on just to promote to her children a radical political agenda.

Do most folks move to home school after having had an issue with a particular school or teacher?

It can be the trigger, but it is not usually a *cause*. There are more and more families home schooling today who have never had a child attend a public or private school. We are privileged to live in a time when home education can be a choice independent of any unfortunate initiating event.

Do families home school because the husband insists? Because the wife insists?

Family unity in the home school choice is almost always an absolute requirement. One spouse can be (and often is) more inclined to home education than another (or begins that way), but if the endeavor is entirely one-sided it's nearly impossible to make home education work – it simply requires too much whole family effort.

Do families home school so their kids won't have access to birth control and sex education programs?

    Kids at home can access birth control and sex education programs – that's called the internet and the drugstore. Kids at traditional schools can opt out of sex education programs and prophylactic distribution.

    Attitudes towards sex and young people (including children) in our public schools are historically atypical, and for some families this figures in to the decision to school at home. It's usually part of a wider picture, though, where the cultural messages the school seems to be promoting are at variance with or in opposition to the messages the family finds healthy.

Perks and Costs

Home education has its benefits and its sacrifices. Families that are particularly enriched by home school benefits or that are willing or able to absorb the costs will be well suited to the change; families with neither of those profiles may have a harder time transitioning to the system.

Is it easier for kids to pursue side talents at home?

If the home program is designed that way, and many are, self-direction is much more possible at home than in institutional schooling.

What kind of flexibility does home schooling afford?

A home educator can vary teaching styles; conform to learning styles; adapt to school during different times of the day or work a schedule around events and opportunities; can alter the school week or the school year, working year round or working intensively and ending the year earlier; can school at a desk, a kitchen table, in trees, on trampolines, at a campsite or in a car; can teach or have the kids learn online or from tutors and mentors or in a co-op; can study all subjects evenly, concentrate on the three Rs, or take a year to really buckle down and study one subject deeply; can study using books, online sources, or activities.

Flexibility is one of the top perks of home educating.

Can you save money in some areas by home schooling?

There can be some savings. The clothes-race can be less intense, with less need to buy lots of new, trendy items. Some school fees can be cut and the cost of transportation if the local school doesn't bus. There tend to be a lot of small little expenses when you attend a traditional school – buying school supplies for the class at the beginning of the year or bringing in food if you're today's "snack mom".

What are the main financial costs of home schooling?

Obviously the biggest financial hit home school families take is loss of income. If one of two parents has to stay home full or part time to teach, that can be a very big income loss. If a single parent has to adjust his or her hours or career expectations (there's only so much time and energy in a day) in order to teach his kids, there's a financial loss.

You also, of course, have to buy all your own materials – textbooks, programs, field trip fees, membership with zoos or museums – that you choose to purchase. If you're not careful, and even if you are, that can sometimes add up. Remember that schools receive approximately $7,000 to $16,000 per student per year to educate a child. Home educators can, through greater efficiency, beat that by a mile – but they can't expect to educate at home without losing money.

Are there any unexpected costs?

New home educators might be surprised to learn there are expenses that aren't directly related to education. In many ways, moving to home school is a lifestyle change and that is reflected in the budget. For example, there is often a jump in transport costs as families engage with co-ops, activities, volunteer jobs, lessons and sports, and trips – the van asks you for gas in ways a school bus never seems to.

Food is another cost that will jump. Kids eat all day, and in school much of that eating (even for the wealthy) is subsidized by the federal government. Feeding three kids three meals a day instead of two (or one) can make a big budget difference, especially for a family where food costs are already a decent percentage of the monthly expenses. Normally, the higher cost also means much higher quality, but that mitigates the pain, it doesn't erase it.

Are there grants or other programs to help with costs?

Some curriculum, textbook, or online school programs may be willing to help families in an immediate crisis situation.

Local home school organizations may be able to put parents in touch with folks with curricula or materials to donate.

The HSLDA does have a foundation whose mission is to financially assist home school groups and sometimes individuals.

Do adults sometimes say hurtful things to kids who are home schooled?

Yes, often accidentally.

There are a number of misconceptions about home education out there, and those who aren't familiar with it sometimes accidentally play into stereotypes. For example, a common question is, "Do you miss your friends?" This is a very strange question to ask, for example, a teenager who has home schooled for ten years. Does she miss kindergarten friends? Does she miss the friends she has now that she saw yesterday? It's also a necessarily hurtful question – if the student has, as the question implies, recently left school and all her friends and is now friendlessly home educated, what can an inquisitor expect in response but a flood of tears? And if the student is a regular home student with a number of close peer relationships, how not to be offended by the assumption that she is unable to make friends without a teacher and a classroom to make it happen?

Occasionally, offense is given intentionally. Most of these offensive adults aren't trying to attack the student – their beef is with the parents. But in their zeal to make their passionate case against home education they target the kids that are, if their argument is correct, the victims of it. A grown woman arguing the superiority of public school socialization to a six year old home student is an irony even the child might catch.

I don't want to be hurtful. What should I not say to a home schooled kid, then? What should I say?

Frankness and thoughtfulness should keep you safe. Know what you don't know, and own up to it – when you ask questions, make them real ones whose answers will inform you, either about home education or about the student herself, not disguised assertions of personal opinion or argument. Consider a moment before speaking, since it's easy to jump into misunderstanding if your conversation is on autopilot. Take feedback – if the young person seems uncomfortable with the subject, pick another one. Understand that many students have had less than ideal conversations with passing adults about their schooling, and they may be on the defensive – the conversation will likely go more smoothly once they realize you aren't trying to interrogate or convert them. Home students are the same as other young people – they often enjoy talking about their lives, their challenges, and their successes. But they can do so only after they feel they are speaking to a sympathetic audience, not folks looking for ammunition to use against their "school", or their family.

Resource Links

Homeschool Legal Defense Association:
http://hslda.org/

List of state departments of education:
http://www2.ed.gov/about/contacts/state/index.html

A history of and case against universal compulsory education in America:
http://www.washingtonpolicy.org/publications/brief/case-against-compulsion

St. John's College great books reading list:
http://www.sjc.edu/academic-programs/undergraduate/seminar/annapolis-undergraduate-readings/

Charlotte Mason site, Ambleside Online:
https://www.amblesideonline.org/

Bartleby literature source site:

http://bartleby.com/

Used book purchase site:
http://www.abebooks.com/

Free audio literature, volunteer-based:
https://librivox.org/

Mortimer Adler sources:
http://www.thegreatideas.org/adlerbio_short.html

Polka Dot Press, Life of Fred books:
http://www.stanleyschmidt.com/FredGauss/index2.html

Murderous Maths site:
http://www.murderousmaths.co.uk/

Well Trained Mind forum:
http://forums.welltrainedmind.com/

Peace Hill Press:
http://peacehillpress.com/

Robinson Curriculum:
http://www.robinsoncurriculum.com/

A Thomas Jefferson Education:
http://www.tjed.org/

Easy Peasy home schooling:
http://allinonehomeschool.com/

Courtship model, *I Kissed Dating Goodbye:*
http://www.joshharris.com/i_kissed_dating_goodbye.php

Sonlight curriculum:
http://www.sonlight.com/

Answers in Genesis, creation science information:
https://answersingenesis.org/

Apologia curriculum:
http://apologia.com/index.asp?proc=pg&pg=1

Ellen McHenry's Basement Workshop:
http://ellenjmchenry.com/

Lincoln Interactive curriculum:
http://lincolninteractive.org/

Math U See:
http://www.mathusee.com/

Singapore Math:
http://www.singaporemath.com/

VideoText:
http://videotext.com/

Saxon Math:
http://www.christianbook.com/page/homeschool/math/saxon-math

Teaching Textbooks:
http://teachingtextbooks.com/

Math Mammoth:
http://www.mathmammoth.com/

A Beka:
http://www.abeka.com/

My Father's World:
http://www.mfwbooks.com/wps/portal/c/homeschool

Milestone books, suppliers of Rod and Staff:
http://www.milestonebooks.com/?rodstaff.com

NaNoWriMo Young Writers Program:
http://ywp.nanowrimo.org/

Rosetta Stone language program:
http://www.rosettastone.com/

Alpha Omega Publications:
http://www.aop.com/

EuroTalk, Talk Now! Language programs:
http://eurotalk.com/us/

Muzzy language programs:
http://www.early-advantage.com/

Berlitz language:
http://www.berlitz.com/

Cambridge Latin Course:
http://cambridgescp.com/Upage.php?p=clc^top^home

AP testing:
https://apstudent.collegeboard.org/home

Christian Liberty Press, books and testing:

http://www.shopchristianliberty.com/about-christian-liberty-press/

Seton testing:
http://www.setontesting.com/

SAT:
https://sat.collegeboard.org/home

Ohio's department of education on the GED, good general info:
http://education.ohio.gov/Topics/Testing/GED

GRE:
http://www.ets.org/gre/

Children of God for Life on vaccines (caution, some graphic photos possible):
http://www.cogforlife.org/vaccine-overview/

Zaner-Bloser:
https://www.zaner-bloser.com/

SchoolTube:
http://www.schooltube.com/

American Astronomical Society:
http://aas.org/

List of cooperative extensions:
http://earthbox.com/cooperative-extension-list

4-H:
http://www.4-h.org/

Audubon Society:
http://www.audubon.org/

National Park Service:
http://www.nps.gov/findapark/index.htm

NPS Junior Ranger Program:
http://www.nps.gov/kids/jrRangers.cfm

Sketch's World math game:
http://www.multiplication.com/games/play/sketchs-world-multiplication

Dover Publications, sign up for samples:
http://store.doverpublications.com/

Numberphile videos:
http://www.numberphile.com/

Periodic Table of Videos:
http://periodicvideos.com/

NASA:
http://www.nasa.gov/

National Geographic Society:
http://www.nationalgeographic.com/

Some museum and institution reciprocity programs:
http://www.astc.org/passport/
http://www.albrightknox.org/join-support/become-a-member/art-museum-reciprocal-network/
http://www.ahs.org/gardening-programs/rap/find/statebystate
http://narmassociation.org/
https://www.aza.org/reciprocity/

Home Science Tools:
http://www.hometrainingtools.com/

Carolina Biological Supply Company:
http://www.carolina.com/

Quality Science Labs:
http://www.qualitysciencelabs.com/

How Stuff Works:
http://www.howstuffworks.com/

DK books:
http://www.dk.com/us/

NOVA:
http://www.pbs.org/wgbh/nova/

The Great Courses:
http://www.thegreatcourses.com/

Usborne books:
http://www.usborne.com/

Cathy Duffy reviews:
http://cathyduffyreviews.com/

Khan Academy:
https://www.khanacademy.org/

CurrClick:
http://www.currclick.com/

University of Dallas home school admission:

http://www.udallas.edu/admissions/homeschool/index.html

MIT home school admissions:
http://mitadmissions.org/blogs/entry/homeschooled_applicants

List of MOOC providers:
http://www.technoduet.com/a-comprehensive-list-of-mooc-massive-open-online-courses-providers/

Coursera:
https://www.coursera.org/

edX:
https://www.edx.org/

Code Avengers learning to code:
https://www.codeavengers.com/

MIT's Scratch coding program:
https://scratch.mit.edu/about/

Practical Homeschooling Magazine
http://www.practicalhomeschooling.com/

Well Trained Mind Forum:
http://forums.welltrainedmind.com/

Scripps National Spelling Bee:
http://spellingbee.com/

Science Olympiad:
http://www.soinc.org/

Mother of Divine Grace School:
http://www.motherofdivinegrace.org/

Seton Home Study School:
http://www.setonhome.org/

Gordon Neufeld and child development:
http://neufeldinstitute.com/blog/author/gordon-neufeld/

Notes

Notes

Notes

Notes

Notes

Notes

Notes

Notes

Notes

Notes